Cobbled Beat

I wish to dedicate this book to the memory of my mother, Elsie, and to my wife, Mary.

© Tony Fletcher 2000

Published by The Bluecoat Press, Liverpool
Book design by March Design, Liverpool
Printed by Manchester Free Press

Front cover
An officer from Mill Street police station returning an escaped sheep back to the abattoir in the 1950s.

Acknowledgements
My grateful thanks go to Liz Wilkinson of the Bluecoat Press for the skilful way in which she edited this book and to Emily Cooper, who typed the manuscript and corrected my grammatical errors.

ISBN 1 872568 72 6

Cobbled Beat

Tony Fletcher
with illustrations by Harold Riley

The Bluecoat Press

Introduction

For much of the twentieth century, each industrial town had its own cobbled beats, with landscapes, accents and characters unique to itself.

During this period, Manchester's boundaries encompassed one of the country's most industrialised areas. Here, in this gloomy and funny spot, I have chosen to write about my two years as a probationary police constable, where things had to be learned the hard way, out at the sharp end, with very little tuition or supervision.

As I wrote, I was determined not to be too economical with the truth about a fascinating era in the Police Service. I wanted to tell what it was like to be a policeman on C Division of the Manchester Police Force, before the Panda car came along to alter the system, and to relate incidents which amused me whilst working in the close-knit communities which have long since disappeared.

I started with the intention of writing a funny book, because, in many ways, working on C Division and meeting such a variety of unusual and colourful characters was funny but, as I progressed, I found that the sad and the violent incidents were inseparable.

Although I have occasionally amalgamated two separate incidents, to make the story more readable, not necessarily recorded events in strict chronological order, very occasionally moved residents from one area to another and altered names so as not to cause embarrassment, this is a reasonably accurate account of my early working life on C Division.

The Rookies

"M2CK to Hotel Tango Two. Come in Tango Two."

Impeded by the volume of traffic and major road repair works, a black Maria slowly threaded its way through the Manchester streets, heading towards the heart of the city.

"M2CK to Hotel Tango Two. M2CK to Hotel Tango Two. Come in Tango Two."

Inside the large prison van, the uniformed driver angrily snatched the handset from its cradle, switched to transmission and, ignoring normal procedure, called out:

"Tango Two to M2CK. I know I'm late, but there's nothing I can do about it. Tell them I'm on my way."

Minutes later, the van nosed its way under the arched gateway of Police Headquarters and came to a halt under the blue sign which hung over the charge office doorway. The driver jumped down and swung open the van's heavy door.

"OK, Sir," he called to the tall, distinguished-looking Police Inspector who was marching across the yard, glancing impatiently at his watch. "Murder coming through town in the rush hour, the traffic was chaotic."

As if also waiting anxiously for their transport to arrive, a group of men, each carrying a brown paper parcel, jostled through the double oak doors of the charge office and childishly climbed into the rear of the vehicle in single file. Whilst they were doing so, the Inspector escorted a young policewoman to the front and gallantly helped her to clamber up into the high cab. Satisfied that she was comfortably settled on the worn leather seat, he carefully closed the door behind her. In contrast to the other men, he tried to act like a gentleman.

At the back of the Maria, the eldest, and also the smallest man in the group, had taken a pace backwards and now joked with the others as they pushed past him. His sense of humour, stance, age and demeanour all proclaimed his years of military experience. Half of those who filed in front of him he addressed as Tosh, the other half as Tish. When all the men had crowded inside, the driver, whilst still holding on to the door handle, managed to push his head into the van.

5

"Crikey! Just like the Black Hole of Calcutta. Everyone comfortable?"

"Comfy? You must be joking, Tosh. If someone farts in here it'll be like a blinking gas chamber."

'Well, nobody fart then. And don't worry, lads, they say that the first two hours are the worst."

Chuckling to himself, he slammed the heavy metal door with such force that it rocked the Black Maria on its chassis, rattling the eardrums of those inside.

A nod from the Inspector and we were on our way. The driver engaged gear and, after reversing the clumsy vehicle in the small yard, he nosed it out through the arched gateway. The loading process had taken no more than two minutes and the Inspector, obviously glad to see the back of us, marched briskly indoors, his duty done.

After less than 30 yards in slow motion, we ground to a halt at the junction of Peter Street, close to the historic scene of the Peterloo Massacre. The driver waited whilst a uniformed constable, positioned on the footpath, strolled into the road, halted the flow of traffic and beckoned him forward. As the van swung in front of him, two fingers were thrust up to the small rear window.

"Up yours, Tosh!"

In the prison van's dark interior, two lines of men sat facing each other on the slatted wooden seats. Tucked under the seats and almost hidden behind the rows of legs, were the brown paper parcels neatly tied with string.

"Roll on 1973," said the joker in a loud voice so that everyone could hear.

I sat with my back resting against the metal side of the van, sandwiched in the middle of a row of five, scrutinising the six men opposite, crunched up shoulder to shoulder. The Maria was designed purely for security, with no consideration given to comfort and we could feel every bump as it lurched along the cobbled streets. 1973 seemed a long way off.

The date was Monday 13 September 1948 and, together with the others, I had just joined the Manchester City Police. We were on our way to begin our basic training at the No1 District Police Training Centre, near Warrington, a journey of some 20 miles. The young policewoman at the front was the only one travelling in anything like style. We wore civilian clothes, the brown paper parcels at our feet contained our uniforms. 1973 would be the earliest we could retire on pension! Most of us had met for the first time an hour or so earlier and now, in the confined space of the overcrowded van, we began to get better acquainted.

I was a 20-year-old from Stockport and on my left was Roy Foxall, another Stockport lad of similar age. Although we had been friends for many years, we had joined the Police Service unbeknown to each other. He had been demobilised from the Royal Marines and I had come from a drawing office, where I had been training as an engineering draughtsman.

I nodded and smiled at the dark-haired, good-looking man sitting opposite. He was about five or six years older than me and was dressed in a dark grey, hand-knitted, polo-necked sweater. He leant forward to offer me a cigarette.

"I'm Bill Sumners," he announced in a soft Scots accent.

We immediately nicknamed him Jock and I was to learn that he was an ex-trawler man from Aberdeen.

"Tony Fletcher; this is Roy Foxall.'

In the Black Maria other men were introducing themselves. We didn't know it then, but once we had completed our training, Jock, Roy and I were earmarked to serve on the same division.

In those days, there were millions of cobblestones between Manchester and Warrington and the prison van seemed to find every one. The wooden slats of the seats impressed ridges into my backside and my back and shoulders ached from the constant collision with the side of the vehicle. The small vent in the roof had long since lost its battle with the tobacco smoke and our friend, the joker, had called out, at least a dozen times, "Enough's enough, for God's sake," when suddenly, we lurched drunkenly round a corner, then another, before finally grinding to a halt. The driver threw open the rear door and we gratefully tumbled out amidst a cloud of blue cigarette smoke.

We had drawn up alongside a concrete parade-ground where a bull-necked, moustachioed Drill Sergeant was waiting to greet us.

"You lot, change into uniform and back on the parade ground in double quick time," he screamed.

"Shite!"

The Canadian drawl came from a tall, ginger-haired lad, who ruefully rubbed his bruises. The Drill Sergeant made no comment, not quite sure whether the remark was addressed at him.

I wasn't very impressed by the Police Training Centre, whose title made it sound grander than it looked. It had been built as a base for the United States Air Force in World War Two and it didn't appear to have changed much on that Monday morning in 1948. Without a war and without aircraft, it looked drab, uninteresting and decidedly uncomfortable but, for 13 weeks, it would have to do.

"Fall in, in two ranks," bawled the Drill Sergeant, when we emerged from the Nissen hut a few minutes later, joking about the cut and style of our new uniforms.

"Trousers too tight about my ruddy chest," joked the smallest man as he strutted out.

I was struggling with the hook and eye fasteners at the neck of my greatcoat.

"I'll help you, Tosh."

"Atten-tion!"

The scream stopped us in our tracks and we had to leave the neck of the greatcoat secured by only one hook and eye.

Some had donned greatcoats and all the men wore closed neck tunics.

Only the young policewoman wore a collar and tie. Unfortunately, it looked as though it had been arranged by a 7-year-old Brownie, who was good at granny knots. The Sergeant immediately marched in front of her and carefully demonstrated how to tie a Windsor knot. She was very attractive and it took him an awfully long time and left her blushing a deep red, much to the amusement of the little joker. As I looked at him more closely, I noticed that over his left-hand breast pocket were two rows of medal ribbons. He didn't look at all like my idea of a policeman and I gained the impression that the war years hadn't been kind to him.

When the Sergeant had spent as much time as he dared adjusting the policewoman's tie, he turned his attention to the rest of us.

"What a bloody shower!" he wailed, making it obvious that he didn't include the policewoman in his assessment.

Most of the men had many years of military experience and, considering that we had merely been weighed for our uniforms and been given no instructions as to the wearing of greatcoats, I felt we looked quite smart.

As I studied the Sergeant, it was easy to see that he'd seen too many war films and was play-acting. Suddenly, his attention became riveted on the tall, ginger-haired lad with the Canadian accent and he marched along the line to stand in front of him, his moustache bristling. But Sullivan, the Canadian, seemed quite unmoved. The Sergeant's eyes sought out his and held them briefly, before dropping slowly down the length of his whistle chain, the row of medal ribbons, the creases in his trousers and finally coming to rest on his brown leather shoes. He appeared nonplussed and stared into the distance as if thinking, "a Yank with brown shoes, what next?"

"You were instructed to attend in black boots," he screamed, "so why in hell's name haven't you done so?"

"I was demobilised in these shoes," replied Sullivan with deep feeling, as though they were the finest shoes which had ever been cobbled. "Besides, I've no black boots."

The Sergeant changed tack.

"Which branch of the Service?"

"Royal Air Force," drawled Sullivan.

"And before that?"

"Winnipeg, Sergeant," adding, as an afterthought, "Canada."

"And you've no black boots?"

"No, Sergeant, none at all," replied Sullivan, still unflustered.

"Well go and bloody well get some and don't report back until you have!"

If this was to be a battle of wills, then it was no contest. Sullivan made a fairly smart right turn, nodded coolly at the Sergeant, smiled at the rest of us and then loped off rather as Gary Cooper might have done. He didn't return with his black boots until Thursday afternoon – three days later.

Shortly after Sullivan's departure, we were joined by eight more recruits; seven from Liverpool and one from Birkenhead. Together, we

8

formed 0 Class. It seemed only fitting that, on his return, Sullivan should be elected our class leader, but his appointment was short-lived. On the parade-ground, it was the duty of the class leader to bring his class to attention, immediately prior to inspection. As a prelude to this, it was necessary to call out his class number in a loud voice. On three consecutive mornings, Sullivan called out "0" in a voice trembling with sexual ecstasy. Most of us thought it amusing, but the Commandant didn't. With a few strokes of the pen, Sullivan was removed as class leader and 0 Class became E Class. Six months later, Sullivan left for Canada. He had booked his passage before joining the bobbies and was merely marking time before sailing home.

Although there was a carefree atmosphere in the classroom during the 13 weeks of basic training, we were kept fully occupied. We learned the elements of criminal law, the Road Traffic Acts, as well as the rudiments of police work. Some of it must have stuck because, more than 50 years later, I can still recite the definition of larceny. Times haven't changed and first aid, civil defence and swimming were all treated as a joke. We all obtained the required first aid certificate and even I, a poor swimmer at best, was awarded a certificate for life saving. My success was largely due to the fact that the person I was elected to save was a powerful swimmer who simply refused to drown.

The Commandant's lecture on fingerprints revealed that he knew as little about the subject as I did about life-saving.

One morning a convoy of lorries took us to a local cinema which had been specially opened to screen an American detective film. The hero summed up detective work as 90% legwork and 10% brainwork. The instructors endorsed the film as being true to life. It needed to be! That, and the fingerprint lecture, was all our CID training!

Of the three hundred or so recruits who passed through the centre, only one failed the course, a Liverpudlian, who didn't make the grade for health reasons. His feet were in such a bad state, that he spent most of his time creeping around the camp in white plimsolls. I spoke to him only once, when he was hobbling painfully across the parade-ground as though his toes were on fire. Surprisingly, when I asked how he was, he complained about his piles.

"Hanging down like a bunch of grapes," he winced, through clenched teeth.

The next week he was gone.

We had time for a lot of sport and amused ourselves with a contest which had no name, but which I particularly remember, because I became the champion. It involved racing along the central corridor of a large Nissen hut. The corridor was about 90 feet long and about three feet wide and gave access to about 25 bedrooms. The race involved two men, starting from different ends, running the length of the corridor and back. The first one home won. As they dashed furiously along, each contestant was encouraged by his own supporters, grouped in the bedroom doorways. The critical part of the race came when the runners met in the centre of the corridor on both the outward and return journeys. Making way for the opposition, or retreating into a doorway, meant a loss of ground and provoked derisive catcalls.

It was a knock-out competition in more ways than one and, after several preliminary rounds, I met Sullivan in the final. Apart from being faster and heavier, I was also considered sufficiently reckless for the betting fraternity to make me the 3-1 favourite. It was a brief contest with no quarter asked or given. We leant forward on our marks, waiting for the blast of the starter's whistle. When it came, Sullivan let out an Indian war whoop and rushed towards me, legs and arms flailing. We clashed halfway and he was left a laughing, tangled wreck on the corridor floor. It was the silliest game I have ever played.

Returning to Manchester, we attended the small training department, at Police Headquarters, for a week's further instruction on local procedures and bylaws. Back within our own domain, training was treated far more seriously – a real preparation for work. During that week, we were presented to the members of the Watch Committee and sworn in as constables. We had finally made it.

Late on Friday afternoon, the tall, slim Inspector announced our postings: Fletcher to C Division as C96, Foxall to C Division as C11 and Sumners to C Division as C49. As the general order was read out, those posted to the same division gathered in small groups, as if already acknowledging the clan system which prevailed.

The young policewoman stood alone. Unlike the men, they were not, in those days, attached to territorial divisions but remained in their own small department at headquarters.

The course had ended and now the real learning process was about to begin. However, before we were allowed to go our separate ways, the Inspector drew us together and addressed us in a serious voice.

"Before I finally dismiss you, I am going to introduce you to Miss Hopkinson, from the Christian Police Association, who has come to tell you something about the movement and also to lead you in prayer." At this point, he raised his eyebrows and continued sternly, "Miss Hopkinson must be treated seriously and with respect. She's a fine old lady and a true friend of the police." He paused, allowing the message to sink in and shifting his gaze from face to face, making eye contact with each of us in turn. "There will be no laughing, no practical jokes and when we come to the Lord's Prayer, you will all join in. Is that clearly understood?"

There was no reply, but it was clear that there had been trouble with previous classes. The warning probably meant more to me than it did to the others. It brought back childhood memories of giggling with my brothers in church, especially during communal prayers. When the Lay Preacher, a Probation Officer in his professional life, realised what was happening, he split us up and I was asked to pump the organ. For two years that was where I sat, by the side of the old organ, leaning on the stout wooden handle, frequently giggling to myself but out of sight of the congregation.

The Inspector left the room to reappear a few minutes later escorting a rather frail old lady in her late 80s. She was well below medium height, bespectacled and expensively dressed in grey, with a mauve hat and black silk choker and she exuded an air of gentility and wealth. They made a strange couple, as they stood in front of us, with the Inspector assuming what he considered the appropriate attitude, by clasping his hands in front of him and arranging his features into an angelic expression.

We dutifully shuffled forward and formed a horseshoe around them. Behind his benign and gentle features, the warning was clearly visible. Opening her prayer book, Miss Hopkinson coughed gently behind her lace handkerchief and then addressed us for several minutes on matters relating to Christianity. Then she asked us to join our hands together and close our eyes in prayer. She began to pray and, every now and then, the Inspector solemnly intoned, "Amen".

She proved to be a true professional, capable of praying for England, as well as, in those days, all her dominions. Identifying her present flock to the Lord, she outlined the dangers and temptations we faced and entered into deep and earnest beseechings on our behalf. She prayed on and on.

Mindful of the Inspector's stern warnings and my own shortcomings, I had decided to detach my mind from the proceedings. But suddenly I was aware of a continuous shaking next to me. I opened my left eye slightly and, squinting sideways, realised that Roy Foxall was about to explode into hysterical laughter. His lips were tightly compressed and his face scarlet. I found myself beginning to lose control and fought to contain myself, to choke back any sound, whilst my body heaved in convulsions, until every bone and muscle began to ache. I pressed my lips together, clenched my teeth, screwed my eyes tightly shut, squeezed my fingers and curled my toes until they went numb. Thankfully, on the verge of losing all control, we were able to gasp out, "Amen" at the end of the Lord's Prayer and Miss Hopkinson remained blissfully unaware of the excruciating predicament in which she had placed us all.

C Division

Roy, Jock and I paraded before the superintendent in charge of C Division the following Monday morning. The briefing was concise: "Welcome to C Division. Today I have arranged for Sergeant Watson to show you round the division. Tomorrow, you'll start work. You won't become policemen overnight, so don't be impatient. Learn to walk before you run. For the next two years you will be on probation, so keep your noses clean."

That was it. The superintendent was a busy man. He didn't bother to dismiss us but picked up his pen and paper and started to write at an incredible speed. After a few moments, with no movement from us, he glanced up.

"You'll find Sergeant Watson in the canteen."

We looked at each other and trooped out of the room, leaving him to his high-speed writing.

Minutes later, Sergeant Watson, a giant of a man, was leading us through the station door into a swirling blanket of white snowflakes, filtering through the grey-green smog. In certain parts of the division, this smog was a semi-permanent feature of the landscape.

"Well now, let's get to know the C Division."

He'd been allocated a day but it was to take me years.

In those days, the city of Manchester was some 12 miles from north to south but perhaps no more than 5 miles wide at best. Like all big conurbations, it had its points of contrast: on its southern side were grand houses built by the cotton barons and rich Jewish families, which had been joined, towards the end of the 19th Century, by small enclaves of reasonably good terraced housing; on its northern side, there were rows and rows of poor dwellings, which ran close to the heart of the city.

But enough of that, for it was on the eastern side that C Division lay. In mediaeval times there had been little more than a few hamlets with, perhaps, a great house or two in extensive grounds positioned here and there. Of course, much of what happens to an area depends on what nature has provided. Here there were rivers and streams – just what was needed to drive factory machinery – a few coal mines, a good quantity of lime and plenty of room to build the never-ending sprawl of terraces needed to accommodate the arriving masses.

By the time I was posted there, the air we had to breathe was a rich amalgam of century old coal dust, the stench from several glue works, coal-gas leaks and the gaseous discharges from several chemical factories. Combined with all this were the smoke and fumes from steel works, wire works, electrical engineering enterprises and a huge railway engine plant. All this, coupled with the worst offender of all, the smoke from thousands of domestic hearths and personal smoking habits, left little room for oxygen and natural sunlight.

Asthma, bronchitis and other chest infections were rife, ensuring long queues at the doctors' surgeries and full employment at the cemeteries.

This description makes it all sound very grim and in many ways it was, but a police division must be judged, in the main, by the people who live there. By any standards, these Mancunians were the salt of the earth, generous, open-hearted and with an attitude to life which made a mockery of both their working and living conditions. Today, television keeps people indoors, when once they would have been standing on their front doorstep, engaged in neighbourly gossip. Being so involved in what went on around them, meant that human kindness abounded in many ways, with local women even acting as midwives and nurses when required.

The scarcity of cars in 1948, meant that most crime was strictly local. Consequently, after a few years of circulating through the beat system, moving every six weeks from beat to beat, one acquired quite a store of knowledge and expertise. Not only were you in constant touch with the ne'er-do-wells, but the local characters were drawn to the uniform, as if by a magnet.

The area of C Division hasn't changed much and covers Levenshulme, Longsight, Ardwick, Chorlton on Medlock, West Gorton, Gorton, Ancoats, Beswick, Bradford Openshaw, Higher Openshaw, Miles Platting and Clayton – one of the most heavily industrialised areas on the planet for most of the 20th century.

In my time, the division was run by a Superintendent, assisted by a Chief Inspector. There were three shifts, or reliefs, as they were called: 6am – 2pm, 2pm – 10pm and 10pm – 6am. Each relief had a Charge Office Inspector and a Patrolling Inspector. There were six sections in the division, each controlled by a Section Sergeant and each section consisted of five beats. Although there were 30 beats in the division, they were numbered 1 – 35. There was no 6, 12, 18, 24 or 30 beat.

What the general public called police stations, were sometimes referred to as section houses – a distinction without a difference. Brunswick Street Section House, situated close to Ardwick Green, accommodated the 1st and 2nd sections and was manned 24 hours a day by a Section House Officer, on each of the three reliefs. Levenshulme Section House did the same for the 3rd section and Gorton Section House for the 4th. The 5th and 6th sections occupied the Divisional Headquarters at Mill Street, Bradford, and were manned throughout the 24 hours by a Station Inspector and a clerk, on each of the three reliefs.

There was a fixed point system. Each beat had four and the beat constable was expected to be at each one in turn at 30 minute intervals during the day and at 45 minute intervals during the night.

When first issued with his uniform, the young policeman was also handed his 'appointments' – not a list of engagements, but items of equipment: notebook, a staff, which most people call a truncheon, snaps or handcuffs, whistle and chain and a leather dog lead, which for some reason no policeman carried, but was perhaps given to him to remind him that the handling of stray dogs was part of his duties!

Each Sergeant and Inspector had his own stick. It was an essential part of his accoutrements and was either specially made, or acquired by grace and favour. Not to be confused with the truncheon, these sticks were between three and four feet long and carried like a walking cane. Often made of ash, but sometimes, and more expensively, of lignum vitae, they are still made at a shop on Great Ancoats Street, Manchester.

The stick was most valuable at night, when it was necessary for the Sergeant and the constable to rendezvous. Should the Sergeant be a little late, or the constable be detained by an incident, the stick would be tapped on the pavement and, under favourable conditions, could be heard over an amazing distance, perhaps as much as a mile. The constable would respond by tapping his staff on the pavement, or flashing his light, if he needed to. All this now appears rather primitive, but in those days, no personal radios were available.

At strategic points on the C Division, there were 30 police boxes, left over from a system which had operated a decade or two earlier. Each had a telephone and a flashing light. If an officer was wanted, the divisional telephonist would cause the box light to flash and a quick and effective response was expected.

When a constable made an arrest, he had no means of summoning assistance directly from a police station, though, of course, he did have his whistle. However, if he blew that, in certain areas of the division, he might only attract a hostile crowd that he could well do without. I only attempted to blow mine once and found it to be clogged up with fluff and tobacco dust. So, in effecting an arrest, the officer had to manhandle the culprit, usually struggling like mad, to the nearest police box, which could be up to a mile away. He had to subdue and hold onto him, whilst opening the box with a key attached to his whistle chain which, in turn, was hooked onto a button of his tunic. He then had to put the prisoner into the police box and, if he had enough breath left, use the telephone to summon the Black Maria. There was a certain knack to the procedure, but tempers were often frayed. I was once attacked by a drunken old lady with an umbrella whilst struggling with a prisoner. I won't repeat what I called her but it only brought on a renewed attack.

Each division had its own CID and plain-clothes officers. On the C Division, the plain-clothes staff dealt with prostitution, obscene publications and the licensing laws. In a way, it served as a training ground for the CID, which dealt with crime, serious and trivial alike. Many a young officer had dreams of joining the CID but, for most, it didn't come quickly, if at all. The work of a CID Officer has always been different from that of a uniformed bobby but it was advantageous to walk the beat for some years if transfer was to be successful. Only by walking the beat can a policeman learn about the preservation of the peace, the maintenance of law and order and, above all, the art of public relations.

At any hour of the day or night, the C Division was manned by upwards of 50 Police Officers, all male, the majority working on the streets. Walking through those grimy, but mainly cheerful communities, most of them cut an impressive figure, creating a stern sense of justice, sobriety and Christian endeavour; men who were not to be meddled with, or taken lightly. In many cases this was an impression deliberately created to mislead.

In 1948, discipline on the division was not only lax, but frequently almost non-existent. A lot of the old policemen, including Inspectors and Sergeants, who had joined the Force in the 1920s and '30s, at a time of massive unemployment, were well above average in both intelligence and physique. Now, they were disillusioned by low pay and poor working conditions, which also included shift work and a six-day week. All this compared unfavourably with other occupations, at a time of full employment. Additionally, the vast majority of the recruits were ex-servicemen, many with five or six years' war experience, who had seen enough discipline and bull to last them a lifetime. Thus, circumstance brought together many supervisors who did not wish to enforce strict discipline and many recruits who had no intention of subjecting themselves to it.

During the war, the city had been blitzed and policemen had joined in the looting of bomb damaged shops and warehouses, setting a dangerous precedent. Three years after the war had finished, many commodities were still strictly rationed and the temptation to steal was ever present. After shops or warehouses had been broken into and entered, many policemen took advantage of the situation and stole butter, sugar, tea, bacon, cigarettes, spirits and nylon stockings. One had to live in that period to even begin to understand why they did it.

Contrary to the police disciplinary code, the majority of officers on the division solicited gratuities, mainly from bookmakers, who in those days were running illegal businesses. One or two officers slept with prostitutes and openly boasted about it. Most officers drank on duty, many heavily and a few, including two Inspectors and four or five Sergeants, were alcoholics.

I will not dwell on these circumstances, except to say that they existed and persisted for the next four years, until four officers, including two Sergeants, were sentenced to long terms in prison after being found guilty of committing crimes on the C. Then, and only then, did the winds of change begin to blow. It was a unique period in the history of the Manchester Police Force and it is very doubtful whether such a culture could still exist today.

Assisting the professional lawmen, was a sprinkling of special constables and a few dedicated lady telephonists. Supernumerary to the division, was a middle-aged lady, K11, who patrolled the main Gorton shopping area at night, checking that all the lock-up property was secure and reporting to the beat constable any unusual light, or suspicious circumstances. She rarely took a night off, was more diligent than many of the officers and, on occasions, would be the only one actually working in the area. Kay was the nearest thing we had to a policewoman.

On the division were three traffic posts or points, as they were known to the public. The busiest by far, controlled by two men working in harmony, was at Ardwick Green, at the junction of five busy roads and criss-crossed by traffic, including trams and trolley-buses. The second busiest was at Belle Vue where, as a safety precaution, the officer climbed into a pulpit, as if preparing for a bible reading. The third was the least popular and it was here, at the T junction of Ashton Old Road and Midland Street, that I had my first taste of traffic duty, within a few days of joining the C and still waiting to be attached to my permanent relief. Although in a dreary and dilapidated area, there was one major attraction; a large brewery, where an allowance could be obtained in both the morning and afternoon.

It was arranged that I should be working 'hours about' with an old copper; one hour on the post, one hour patrolling Ashton Old Road. Being new, I was on first. After a few minutes instruction from my elderly colleague, I was on my own. Between 8.30am and 9.30am, it was fairly busy, as traffic made its way into the city. The last few minutes of my first stint was spent under the watchful eyes of the old copper, before he strode out into the road to relieve me.

"Not bad, Ninety-six, but learn to relax a bit more and for Christ's sake don't stop the railway horses."

I nodded whilst removing the white sleeves.

"Sorry about that, I just wasn't thinking. They've enough to do pulling the carts, without any additional stopping and starting."

He seemed surprised that I should have considered the horses' welfare. Obviously such a thought had never entered his head.

"No, it's not that, Ninety-six," he said earnestly. "When you stop 'em, the buggers tend to shit and when it dries out, it blows all over your uniform."

At 10.30am it was my turn to relieve the old copper, which I did promptly, confident of my ability to look after the post. With a last reminder about the railway horses, he skived off, not to reappear until 1pm.

At 11.30am, with no sign of a relief, I was quite happy to carry on. It was a fine day, if somewhat cold and this was a new experience for me. Then a heavily-laden coal lorry, groaning and creaking under a mountain of coal, came slowly towards me from the railway sidings. As it came nearer, the driver's mate indicated their intention of turning sharply into Midland Street, by thrusting a grimy arm through the nearside cab window. I was already giving precedence to traffic moving in their direction, so casually signalled the driver to proceed and then stepped back a few feet, to allow him more space to negotiate the narrow junction. Even at 5mph he was a little too 'quick, for suddenly a hundredweight of nutty-slack came avalanching down the mountain and deposited itself in a steady stream around my feet.

"So much for the old copper and his dried horse manure," I thought. Fortunately, in the winter of 1948, there was a shortage of coal. Within minutes, the door of a nearby house opened and an old lady appeared, complete with bucket and shovel. Whilst I held up the traffic and made a fuss of her, she quickly scooped up the coal and tidied up the post. At 12.30pm, still with no signs of relief, only light traffic on the road and feet like blocks of ice, I was beginning to lose my concentration and my arms jerked about like a robot.

Approaching along Midland Street, was a gaily-coloured baker's van, whose driver was indicating his intention to turn right. I turned sideways onto him, halted the traffic moving along Ashton Old Road, beckoned him on and stepped back a pace, to allow him to pass in front of me. Gazing about absent-mindedly, I was suddenly aware that there was something amiss. Out of the corner of my right eye I caught sight of the van heading straight towards me. Jumping around in alarm, I saw the driver steering with only his left hand, maintaining his course, as if aiming to run me down. I leapt out of his path and angrily spun round to face the driver, who had reduced his speed to a crawl.

"What the hell's going on?" I started to shout, when suddenly an arm stretched through the cab window and deposited a steaming hot meat and potato pie on my outstretched hand.

"Straight from th'oven. See you tomorrow," he called out, as he accelerated away.

I wasn't going to work the traffic with a hot meat and potato pie in one hand, so, seconds later, I was knocking on the old lady's door.

"Would you like a hot pie for your dinner, luv?"

Naturally she accepted, but looked at me rather oddly, as if meeting a new breed of policeman.

At 1pm the old shirker returned, looking decidedly more cheerful and reeking of peppermints.

"Got engaged with a crime report," he lied. "Any problems?"

"No, everything's normal," I replied, truthfully, as it turned out.

So what could be considered normal on the C Division? Through the eyes of a 20-year-old recruit, 'normal' was sometimes amusing, occasionally bizarre, at times, totally outrageous. Certainly not in accordance with the book but, amazingly, something which left the residents feeling secure and in good hands.

Guard Cat – 35 Beat

Wreathed in an almost perpetual fog, in an area between Ancoats and Miles Platting, lay 35 Beat; a tiny square of densely-populated land, with a triangular appendage on its southern flank, called Tripe Island. The smallest and most isolated beat on the division, it lay almost forgotten under the shadows of two towering grey gasometers, directly in line with the gaseous discharges from the nearby chemical factories

It was a difficult beat to work; too little to do but too isolated to be able to creep away and seek interest elsewhere. Dirty and smelly, it was not a place to idle away the time in any comfort.

Close to Tripe Island was the Red Rec; an open area of shale wasteland, where many of the local lads played football. They approached the game with vigorous aggression and on Saturday afternoons it was not a place for the faint-hearted.

Running parallel to the ground, was one of the larger chemical factories, a long, low-lying building, from which the night shift discharged chemical waste into the atmosphere. Without warning, in the early hours of the morning, a grey-green cloud of gas would billow across the Red Rec, reminiscent of the gas attacks of the First World War. Afterwards, the atmosphere was so murky, that distant figures appeared as ghostly outlines emerging through the mist.

After three months in the area, helmet badges became so tarnished that they had to be replaced. At the central stores, the storekeeper would note the badge's condition, glance at your collar number and call out knowingly, "Thirty-five Beat, eh?" even though he had never worked on C Division.

Nobody wanted to work on the beat but the character and resilience of its residents more than compensated for the area's shortcomings. It was there that I first met Sarah Goodchild, an old lady I was to get to know quite well. It was on a Sunday morning in January, my first day on my first regular beat, 35 Beat; the one they gave to the rookies. It would be mine for six weeks, a fortnight on each of the three reliefs. "Start here, lad, and things can only get better," the Sergeant had said consolingly.

My alarm clock woke me at 3.40am and, after preparing and eating a cooked breakfast, I cycled the 10 miles along cobbled roads to eventually parade at Mill Street at a 5.45. To start work, I had then to walk through 33 Beat which was not pretty either, including as it did, a coal-pit and a power station. The route also included a wireworks, a chemical factory, a rubberworks, a knacker's yard, two or three rows of shops, a park, a polluted river and a cemetery.

Even so, by 11 o'clock I was thinking that the 10 mile cycle journey had been the best part of the morning and was looking forward to the return trip home. "Anywhere but this place," I thought to myself, as I ambled slowly across the Red Rec.

I was wearing a greatcoat, my cape felt like a lead-weight slung across my left shoulder, the band of my new helmet pressed into my forehead, my feet ached and I was fed up to the back teeth with, to borrow an old Stockport expression, simply pawning about. I had been pawning about for five hours, hardly meeting a soul. Nowhere to go, nothing to do and still another three hours left of the shift.

Wandering through a rickety set of goalposts, then hitching my cape more firmly onto my shoulder, I headed disconsolately towards Tripe Island. Now there was a place that dreams were made of! A small, triangular-shaped area containing a dozen or so streets of terraced houses. Along its base ran Hulme Hall Lane; busy, narrow and dirty. Guarding its perpendicular was the canal; smelly, polluted, junk-ridden and long since disused. Sealing off any possible escape route across its curving hypotenuse, was a double set of railway lines, along which a continuous stream of engines and trucks rattled noisily. To the casual observer, daytime social life consisted almost entirely of watching the slow-moving funeral processions, wending their way along Hulme Hall Lane towards Phillips Park Cemetery. As there were no pubs in the island area, nightlife was non-existent.

I wandered along each of its mean little streets, with no other purpose than to kill a little time. A door opened in one of the terraces and an elderly lady came out onto her front doorstep. Her hair was done up in a bun and she was wearing a black shawl across her shoulders, one of the few I can remember seeing in the post-war period. She watched me with interest and waited until I was level with her before she spoke.

"What time is it, Sir?" she asked politely.

I smiled at the thought of an 80-year-old addressing a mere 20-year-old like myself in such a way, simply because of a uniform. I glanced at my watch.

"Twenty past eleven, love," I replied and then chatted with her for a few moments; the only two people astir on Tripe Island. I was aware that she was weighing me up, as the saying goes.

"Dust want a cuppa tea, Sir?"

"It'd certainly go down well, love. It's a bit parky this morning."

Following her into the parlour and taking off my helmet, I sat down next to a large oak table, covered in heavy green chenille. Re-examining me without my helmet, she exclaimed,

"Why, you're nobbut a lad!"

I smiled broadly.

"That's right, love, nobbut a lad dressed in a man's suit."

She cackled pleasantly, amused by my imitation of her accent.

"Now, I didn't mean it that way."

As she went to make the tea in the kitchen, I looked around the room. It was clean and comfortable but no more. It was a time of austerity and her home was typical of many I would encounter. The furniture was old but solid, a coal fire burned in the grate and on the mantelpiece a large wooden clock ticked away solemnly. I checked the clock against my watch and it showed the correct time. The old lady had merely stopped me to enter into conversation and, like me, she was seeking to pass the time. I undid the buttons of my heavy greatcoat, released the hooks and eyes on my tunic collar and gratefully stretched my legs towards the fire; I would have taken my boots off, if I had dared!

On either side of the clock stood a pair of identically framed sepia-coloured photographs, which appeared to have been taken in the same studio, at the same time. Each featured a soldier dressed in a First World War uniform; young, pleasant-looking lads, who bore a strong resemblance to each other. I was still looking at them when the old lady walked back in, carrying two cups and saucers, which she placed on the table in front of me.

"Tea's mashing; only be a minute."

I nodded my head slightly towards the photographs.

"Are they your sons?" I asked, drawing my legs in towards me. Suddenly it didn't seem right to be making myself too much at home.

She moved across to the mantelshelf.

"Aye, both of them," she sighed, carefully removing the one on the left-hand side of the clock and lovingly polishing it with her apron, before handing to me. "Harold, the eldest lad, joined up in 1914. Didn't come through," she whispered softly, "killed near Wipers (Ypres) in 1917." She came and stood behind me, looking over my shoulder, whilst I examined the photograph. "He was the clever one," she added gently. "Would have gone places that lad would." Realising that I was at a loss for words, she added slowly, "never mind, that's all in the past now."

After replacing the photograph, she took down the other frame, which she also lovingly polished before handing it to me. "Sam," she said proudly. "He was the second one. Joined up with his brother. They went into town with their friends and joined the Manchester Pals Regiment on the same day." She again came to peer over my shoulder, adopting the same stance as before. "Different as chalk and cheese them two. Sam was a right harum scarum devil, but everyone loved him."

I looked closely at the photograph, not daring to ask the question that was uppermost in my mind.

"He looks a rum lad, love," I said truthfully.

As she replaced the photograph, she studied it wistfully, warming her shins on the fire with her back to me.

"Wounded and gassed on the Somme he was. Came back in 1916 a changed man. Never went back to France after that. Spent a lot of time in hospital and was then discharged from the army. Died in 1935. Pension place said it was natural causes. Natural causes!" she scoffed. "He were a big strong lad when he joined up. Came back from France after being wounded in't chest and shellshocked. He died when he were 40 and pension place called that natural causes. Fair makes you weep, don't it? Penny-pinching devils."

I agreed with her. She had accepted that both had died for their country, but found it insulting to be told that her youngest son had died of natural causes. With a long sigh she went back into the kitchen and, returning with the teapot, she started to pour.

"Sugar?" she asked.

"Only if you've got it to spare," I replied, mindful of the rationing.

She sat down opposite me and scrutinised me as she passed me my tea, just as she had done on the front doorstep. Whatever it was she was seeking, she obviously found, for she asked me quickly,

"Would you like a piece of Christmas cake? I've made it myself. It's all good stuff – none of your shop bought rubbish."

"I'd love a piece, Ma," I replied.

For some reason I chose to address her that way and she seemed to like it.

She brought out a Macintosh's Quality Street tin of pre-war vintage and took out an iced Christmas cake, decorated with holly bush and plastic robin. Even though it was January, only one small piece had been removed. She cut a thick wedge and proudly handed it to me.

"Try that and tell me what you think."

I took a large bite, conscious that she was waiting anxiously for my reaction.

"Delicious," I said appreciatively, through a mouthful of almond paste and icing.

She smiled contentedly – both the cake and I had passed the test.

"Wash the currants and stone the raisins, that's part of the secret," she disclosed. "After that, it all depends on whether you can bake or not."

She continued to look at the cake rather sadly.

"I've got three daughters who visit me regularly and look after me well." Then, as she put the cake back in the tin, she added, "three good girls they are." Tears were glistening in her eyes as she turned to face me, "but somehow it's nice to have a lad back in th'ouse again."

I finished my tea and cake and glanced up at the clock between the two photographs. I buttoned up my greatcoat and reached for my helmet.

"I'll have to be off now, Ma, I'm due to make a call at the police box."

She showed me to the front door and stood there looking at me wistfully.

"Do call again. I'll be glad to see you anytime you're passing and that Christmas cake's got to be finished off."

She opened the door and stood looking at the houses opposite. When she turned to face me, I was wearing my helmet and she immediately reverted to calling me sir. She spread out her arms, as if taking in the nearby streets.

"Nice little place to live in this is, Sir. I was born in the next street and came to live in this house shortly after I got married. Never wanted to live anywhere else. They call it Tripe Island, tha knows, and in summer tha sometimes gets the Blackpool breezes blowing through here. Hard to believe isn't it, Sir? Blackpool breezes on Tripe Island, but it's true nevertheless."

My nose was wrinkling, and my eyes smarting from the chemicals in the atmosphere. Blackpool was more than 50 miles away. I took a couple of sniffs of the sulphur-laden air.

"No, I'm sure you're right, Ma," I said, as I adjusted my cape on my shoulder and started to stroll away.

"Now don't forget, Sir," she called after me, 'there'll always be a piece of cake waiting for you."

Possibly the Sergeant had been correct when he had remarked that things could only get better; the job might not be quite as bad as I had thought earlier that morning. In my first few hours on a regular beat I had discovered the secret of serving happily on the C. The remedy was simple. Forget the industrial landscape, ignore the smoke, smells and shabbiness of many of its districts and concentrate on the people. Get to know the inhabitants and try to understand them. It wasn't always easy, but it was certainly rewarding.

During my first spell on the beat, I called on Sarah Goodchild almost daily and the Christmas cake was polished off in no time. Eventually, however, I was only able to call on her occasionally.

It was six years before I was selected to work the beat again on a regular basis and only then because an Inspector with a twisted sense of humour, whom I had recently upset, decided to take me down a peg or two and put me right back where I had started.

By this time, I was married and my wife was expecting her first child and I knocked on the familiar door, intending to pass on the good news. A young woman holding a child in her arms answered and I knew instinctively that old Sarah had died.

"Good morning," I said, lamely, "I used to call on Mrs Goodchild and have a cup of tea with her."

The young woman looked at me and, hoisting the baby to her other shoulder, told me that old Sarah had died the previous year. I nodded.

"I guessed as much the moment you opened the door."

"I'll make you a cup of tea," she volunteered willingly.

"No thanks, love. It's kind of you to offer but I'm a bit pushed for time at the moment."

For a policeman to have tea with an old lady is one thing, but to have tea with a young married woman is quite another!

I walked slowly away and smelt the air; plenty of chemical smells, but still no trace of the famous Blackpool breezes. I smiled to myself as I recalled my first meeting with Sarah. I'm not a deeply religious person but it would be nice to think that she had her two lads about th'ouse once again. She'd like that.

Five weeks after my first meeting with old Sarah, it was a bitterly cold Saturday afternoon on the Red Rec. I strolled across to the football pitch where a local Derby was due to be played, or fought, as the case may be. There was a touch of fog and drizzle in the air and the early signs were that the game was going to develop into a battle royal. Most of the players, clad in either a blue or red strip, had been warming up in the nearby pubs, which doubled as their changing rooms. The nearest thing to facilities on the Red Rec was a brick-built public urinal which stood in one corner. The players were either clustered in small groups by the goalposts, or else trotting off to the urinal for a spot of last minute relief.

Occupying the centre spot was the referee, a leather football trapped under his left foot, engaged in consultation with the linesmen. Close to the touchline the two trainers were checking their medical supplies. Aware of the game's importance to the local community, the district's sports reporter was hurrying towards the pitch, trailing a heavily laden photographer in his wake. Once there, he wasted no time in formalities but called out in a loud voice:

"Blues over here for a team photograph, please."

Keen to get their picture in the local rag, the Blues' forward line knelt down with a football in front of them, whilst the rest of the team, the referee, the trainer, the officials and anyone else who could get in on the act, gathered behind them. In front of them, the Reds gathered, offering advice and hurling good natured insults whilst waiting their turn.

"Smile, please!"

Ten of the Blues managed an agreeable grin. However, their big balding centre half, a man who even the spectators feared, could only produce a sneer as he curled his lips back and tried to look pleasant.

Not content with this, the reporter held up the proceedings by trying to coax the giant.

"Big smile now, Frank." The top lip curled back even further, producing nothing more favourable than a threatening leer. "For God's sake, Frank, can't you do better than that?"

The Reds' Captain intervened with some expert advice.

"Just let him kick the photographer in the goolies and then watch him laugh his socks off."

At this, even big Frank managed to produce the long-awaited grin. After the photography session, the reporter spotted my uniform on the fringe of the crowd and approached me with a few well chosen words of advice.

"Good afternoon, Officer," he whispered conspiratorially, with his back to the gathering spectators. "Could be a rough game this afternoon. If I were you I'd wander off before the GBH starts."

It was easy to take heed as I had a beat to work. So, before the referee started the game, I opted for another trek around my territory, arriving back at the Red Rec shortly before half-time. Standing by the reporter's side, I discovered that it was still a goalless draw, with injuries almost even on either side.

After a few minutes, I found myself admiring the speed and courage of the Reds' right winger who, in the circumstances in which the game was being played, was running far too fast for his own safety. A few minutes later, he received the ball deep in his own half and came haring towards us at breakneck speed, with the ball at his feet. He whizzed past, a blur of red and white but, coming across the frozen shale to intercept him, was big Frank. After what was more of a collision than a tackle, the speedy winger was violently upended and, when next seen, was airborne, travelling horizontally in an entirely different direction from the one in which he had been running. After about 10 yards, he crashed to the ground and tobogganed on his stomach and knees, with his legs bent back in the air, across 20 yards of red shale. Followed by a row of eyes, he finally slid to a standstill on the next pitch, without the referee even being aware of his absence.

The trainer, a stocky little man, dressed in oil-stained dungarees and a flat cap, chased after him, holding a bottle of water and a sponge. He helped the lad to a sitting position and allowed him two gulps of the water. Pouring the rest of the icy fluid onto the sponge, he pulled open the elasticated top of his shorts and slapped the dripping mass straight onto the youngster's private parts. Either the water had been specially imported from Lourdes, or the trainer was a miracle worker in disguise, because the winger leapt to his feet like a scalded cat and dashed back to the field of play as if nothing had happened. With a pint of icy water dripping from his shorts, he waited close to the touchline for the ball to be passed out to him. I thought he had shown remarkable courage. Nowadays, a professional player would have been out of action for a month. I was just about to congratulate him, when I found that his captain held a different view.

"Don't fart about there on the touchline, Alfie," he yelled. "Come into the bloody middle and get stuck in like the rest of us."

□ □ □ □

"Produce appointments!"

At the sound of the Inspector's voice, the ten constables clustered round the long high desk in the parade room, withdrew a few paces and brought their legs to something like attention, whilst their hands were thrust out in front. In each left-hand was a notebook and snaps, in the right-hand, the truncheon. The ritual of producing appointments was held each time we paraded for duty. The Inspector and the two Section Sergeants marched through the gap provided and the Inspector placed a heavy journal on the desk in front of him. He glanced at the men.

"Put 'em away," he muttered.

Producing a pair of spectacles from a case, he began to study the journal. The two Sergeants flanking him each looked at their sections, one critically, one benignly.

I replaced my notebook in my left-hand tunic pocket, my snaps in my watch pocket and my truncheon into its own special pocket, where it hung comfortably behind my right thigh. Before parading, I had already made a note of lighting-up time, the mode of working, listed both the stolen and recovered vehicles and recorded those things which required special attention on 35 Beat. All the Inspector had to do now, was to bring us up to date with events which had occurred in the proceeding 24 hours.

He removed his spectacles and announced:

"I've got a message from the DO."

In those days, in Manchester, no one referred to the CID other than as the DO (Detective Office).

"The Afternoon Man has started to operate again." This remark produced a buzz from the men, which the Inspector quickly silenced, merely by waving his spectacles up and down. "I want every beatman to give special attention between 6pm and 9pm each evening." He again consulted the journal. "Let me remind you – he's about thirty-five to forty; height, between five foot seven to eight, medium build, brown hair, flat cap pulled low over the eyes, wears gloves, said to be agile. Breaks into dwelling-houses, likes end-terraces, houses or shops, operates up to 9pm and is usually most active between 7pm and 9pm, when he'll be working under the cover of darkness. Breaks a pane of glass in rear window, releases catch, climbs through, puts the snick down on the front-door lock, so that he won't be surprised if occupier returns home, steals cash and small valuables, leaves by rear door, operates alone and has now committed more than a hundred and twenty offences. Never operates after 9pm, so he's obviously an old lag who knows the difference and doesn't want a conviction for burglary."

In those days there was a distinct difference between house-breaking and burglary. To commit burglary one had to break into and enter a dwelling-house at night time, between 9pm and 6am. It was considered to be a more serious offence than housebreaking and carried a heavier sentence. Knowing this, the Afternoon Man confined his activities to the afternoon or evening. The Inspector was unable to ask us to pay special attention during the afternoon period, as we would all be engaged at, or close to, our school crossing points.

No comment was made by the ten beatmen. Special attention would be paid, but it would be more in hope than in expectation. For ten men to keep an eye on the thousands of terraced houses on the fifth and sixth sections, was a mission impossible.

For the greater part of that evening, I wandered through countless back passageways, disturbing nothing more than the occasional dog or cat, as it was too early for courting couples. Shortly after 9pm, I emerged from a passageway and noticed the police box light blinking in the distance. To my annoyance, the Afternoon Man had struck on my beat. I made my way to a small corner-shop, where the elderly shopkeeper was shining a torch down the side of the blind covering the display window. He was attempting to peer into his premises through the small gap between the window and the blind.

"Mr Jackson?"

He spun round.

'Aye, that's right, Officer. Catch is down on the front door and we can't get in this way. We'll have to go round the back."

He was obviously of a nervous disposition and shone the torch into every corner as he led me down the side street and into his backyard. The Afternoon Man's trademarks were all there to see and the crime had been committed either in the evening, or during the afternoon, when, as it had been half-day closing, the Jacksons had been visiting friends. All I needed now was to take down details for my report but it wasn't to be as easy as that, as the thief had caused considerable disruption to the household. We passed through the scullery and into the living-room, where Mrs Jackson, a large motherly figure, impressive in her jewelled spectacles, was hanging over a parrot's cage.

"Flippin' Nora! Flippin' Nora! Flippin' Nora!" screeched the agitated bird.

"Shush, Polly, shush, Polly," cooed Mrs Jackson.

"Flippin' Nora! Flippin Nora!"

"He's upset, Polly," Mrs Jackson informed me unnecessarily, as she draped a large piece of old blackout curtain material over the parrot's cage in an attempt to calm it. But Polly screeched even more loudly and she was forced to remove the cover.

I glanced at my watch – 9.15pm – I would have to be quick, as I had to walk to Mill Street Station to complete a crime report, before taking a long bus journey home, requiring three connections.

"Right, Mr Jackson, your full name please?"

"Stuart Jackson, Officer."

"Age?"

"Sixty-five, next."

"Occupation?"

"Electrician cum shopkeeper."

"What's been stolen?"

"The shop float which was kept in a biscuit tin in the sideboard."

"Anything else?"

"I haven't been in the shop yet. I don't know if anything's missing there."

"We'd better go and check then."

Mrs Jackson broke off from comforting the parrot and looked at me anxiously through her jewelled spectacles.

"I'm afraid he can't get in, Sir. The guard cat's acting up."

"Guard cat?"

"Aye, guard cat," confirmed Mr Jackson. "I keep him in't shop at night time, or when we're out. Better than any dog. Burglar must have been in't shop and got him wound up. He's not usually so difficult."

My curiosity was aroused.

"I'll need to know what's been stolen, Mr Jackson."

"We'd best go and have a look then, Officer, though I must tell you, I don't like it. I don't like it one bit when he's like this. He's not a full shilling tha knows."

We approached the curtained door which separated the living room from the shop and Mr Jackson drew back the curtain to peer into the darkened room.

"Seems quiet enough, he's settled down a bit," he whispered.

Furtively he opened the door a few inches and, carefully inserting his arm into the narrow gap, started groping about for the light switch. I peeped gingerly over his shoulder.

"Keep your eyes covered, Officer."

He was keeping his face firmly behind the door when suddenly, as he flicked the light on, all hell broke loose.

"Jump back, quick," he blurted out, as he withdrew his arm and slammed the door shut.

"Flippin' Nora. Flippin Nora!" screeched the parrot at the sudden alarm.

As we drew back the curtain again, we were able to look into a well-lit shop. Circling the room at incredible speed, almost bouncing off the walls and ceiling, was a large striped tomcat. It was like perpetual motion as he leapt from wall to wall, using the shop counters as a springboard. Even through the closed door we could hear him hissing and spitting. His claws were stretched out like talons and his wide open mouth revealed his menacing fangs.

I had seen enough and as far as the list of stolen property was concerned, I wasn't going to press the issue. However, Mr Jackson had seen it differently.

"I'll have to get him out now, or he'll mess me shop up from top to bottom."

He grabbed a sturdy dining chair by the back rail and held the four legs out in front of him like a lion-tamer.

"Open back door, mother," he called, and Mrs Jackson left her position by the parrot's cage to oblige. "Now open shop door, Officer."

I obliged and Mr Jackson advanced into the shop using the chair as a shield.

"Flippin' Nora," he yelled, as a bundle of striped fur whistled past his head. "Get back, you swine! Gerrout of it! Gerrout of it!" He backed into the shop, sweeping the chair from side to side, whilst keeping his head well behind the seat. "Gerrout of it! Gerrout of it!" he kept shouting.

By this time, the cat was really excited, crossing and recrossing the room at lightning speed, usually at about head height. Perhaps it felt and smelt the fresh air, for suddenly, still hissing and spitting, it shot past me like a rocket, straight through the back door.

"Flippin' Nora! Flippin Nora!" gasped Mr Jackson and Polly in unison.

After all this commotion, it was still only 9.20pm but, by the time I had completed the report, it would be 10.30pm.

"I'll get a detective to call in the morning," I told them. "Perhaps you'll let him know if anything's been stolen from the shop, though I very much doubt it."

Three months later, the Afternoon Man was caught. His name, too, was Jackson.

That's how we do it! – 8 Beat

"Education – that's what working people should be concentrating on – education. Thirty years ago we never had the opportunities that young people have today."

Tommy Alker strode along Hyde Road, Ardwick, between Roy Foxall and myself. It was a bitterly cold afternoon but sunny and Tommy's breath was emerging in small clouds as he spoke. Roy was on 7 Beat, which lay to the west of Hyde Road, I was on 8 Beat, which lay to the east and Tommy Alker was the Section Sergeant.

"Aye, if there's one thing you can thank this Socialist Government for, it's the opportunity. Both my lads will go on to university, I'll see to that," announced Tommy proudly, his stick tapping the pavement at every stride.

Big, bluff and barrel-chested, this Wigan born ex-collier was a man who really cared, particularly for the young. He was fair to young probationary constables, which was more than some Sergeants and we felt particularly secure in his company. He also enjoyed a pint, both on and off duty and was prone to share the experience with us. Today he was in excellent form and only stopped talking long enough to draw breath, or to listen.

"What were you doing before you joined the bobbies, Number Eleven?" he asked Roy.

"Royal Marines, Sarge. I joined on demob."

"What about you, Ninety-six?"

"Training to be a draughtsman, Sarge."

Tommy maintained his pace but swivelled his head to stare at me, as though he hadn't heard correctly.

"Have you done the right thing, son? Better jobs than the bobbies you know and working in a drawing office is one of them."

I shrugged and answered him truthfully:

"I was a square peg in a round hole – not cut out for engineering."

We walked along steadily, his stick tapping out a gentle rhythm on the footpath.

"Well, make sure you take the promotion exams at the first opportunity. Don't settle for working a beat all of your service, like some people do," he warned, seriously, "and that goes for the pair of you."

He turned his head to include Roy in the warning.

"Not one for paperwork," smiled Roy. "I'll leave that to Ninety-six, his pen's better than mine."

After only a few weeks, we had broken the habit of years and were addressing each other by number.

Discussing the pros and cons of education and the Socialist system, we covered another half mile or so, before arriving at the Fenians Arch, a low and ugly bridge which carried the railway across Hyde Road. Here, at this miserable spot, close to one of its grimy stone pillars, we stopped to chat for a few moments, before going our separate ways. But gloomy and miserable as it was, this spot now linked together the only two Manchester Police Sergeants whose portraits had been painted in oil. I was now in the company of one and close to the ghost of the other.

Some eight years earlier, Tommy Alker had been awarded the British Empire Medal for bravery during the Manchester blitz. Typically, he never spoke of it. The first time I became aware that he had been so honoured, was years later, when I saw the portrait and inscription. The beautifully-framed picture, commissioned by a grateful authority, was gathering dust in a cellar at Police Headquarters. So did the police honour its brave!

The other Sergeant was Charles Brett who, on the 18 September 1867, was murdered at the very spot on which we were standing. He was shot in the head whilst escorting two Fenian prisoners, Colonel Kelly and Captain Deasy, from the Manchester Courts to Belle Vue Prison, where they were to be detained. Hence the name now given to the railway arch.

The story illustrates the length of time that the Irish problem has plagued the citizens of Manchester.

Kelly and Deasy, both veterans of the American Civil War, had been sent to Manchester to reorganise and ginger up the city's branch of the Fenian Movement. Within days of their arrival, they had been arrested, surprisingly, considering the purpose of their visit, for loitering in Shudehill!

Whilst the horse-drawn prison van was conveying them to the prison where they had been remanded, it was ambushed under the arch by upwards of 30 Irishmen, some of them armed. Minutes later, whilst they were releasing Kelly and Deasy, Sergeant Charlie Brett was fatally shot in the head.

After being concealed in two coffins at a local undertaker's, Kelly and Deasy successfully fled to France, but not before three Irishmen had been arrested and charged with the murder of Sergeant Brett. In the November of that year, William O'Meara Allen, Michael Larkin and William O'Brien were publicly hanged outside the walls of the New Bailey Gaol. At the trial, they claimed that the shot which killed Brett had been aimed at the lock which held the van door secure and that his death was accidental. After their execution they became known as the Manchester Martyrs and to commemorate their deaths, a procession and public service is still held each year by members of the Irish community.

If their account of the shooting was true, then there may have been reasonable doubt that the accused had killed Brett with malicious intent, an important ingredient in a charge of murder and they could have been found guilty of the lesser charge of manslaughter. However, many shots were fired during the incident and there can be little doubt where public sympathy lay. Throughout the murky November night of their execution, vast crowds gathered outside the walls of the prison, singing Rule Britannia and then they danced in the streets.

Standing under the Fenians Arch, little did I know that 26 years later and 108 years after the killing of Sergeant Brett, IRA terrorists would again be waging a bombing and shooting campaign in Manchester and yet another Police Officer would be counted amongst its victims.

I mention this now as a matter of pride in the way in which members of the Police Force dealt with this emergency but, before returning to the present, I would like to mention pride again, because in some form or other it affects us all.

To maintain his image, it is essential that the policeman has pride in himself, his appearance and, above all, in the Service he represents. As old heads do not grow on young shoulders and pride usually comes before a fall, the image is frequently, if briefly, tarnished and this pride dented, usually because of the most trivial of incidents.

An officer could be patrolling the district's main shopping street on a summer's day, walking erect with a measured stride, head held high, only to lose his helmet by colliding with a shop sunblind lowered less than the statutory eight feet above the footpath! Members of the public always found this amusing and it added to the young officer's discomfort if the street was crowded and he happened to be using his helmet for carrying eggs, or tomatoes, intended for his refreshments. Some trades or professions have lunch breaks, policemen take refreshments.

A young friend of mine, a strapping six-footer named Jack, lost some pride when he was required to have words with one of the local characters, a mentally-retarded, three foot six inch midget who, sick of having his leg pulled, had started swearing at a group of housewives. Arriving at the scene and in order to maintain the peace, Jack crouched down to counsel him on his behaviour. Whilst off balance, and in a crouched position, the midget uppercut him and sent him sprawling across the footpath. Even though Jack won the rematch and bore the midget home by the scruff of his neck, he was the talk of the district for weeks.

Embarrassment is not only the preserve of young and inexperienced policemen, as I was to discover in circumstances so unusual, that I shall never forget them. Standing under Fenians Arch, Tommy Alker was still holding forth about education and the old days, competing for our attention with the noise of trains rumbling overhead.

"Down the blasted pit at fourteen; working all the hours God sent ..." He was suddenly interrupted by the sight of a very agitated woman, risking life and limb as she dodged between the traffic, intent on crossing the busy road to speak to us. Tommy jumped into the carriageway, stick outstretched, slowing the traffic and allowing her to reach us in safety.

"Steady on now," he shouted, "I don't know what it's all about, but there's no point in killing yourself."

"It's the kids, Sergeant," she panted breathlessly, her spectacles steaming up from the exertion. She took them off and peered at us shortsightedly. "You'd better go and have a look at the school. The little sods are pulling it to pieces." After gasping out this information, she paused and leant forward, almost bent double, clutching at the knot of her headscarf. "Do me heart no good, this won't. I've rushed all the way to find you. There's hundreds of the little sods and they're running riot." The children she referred to were on school holiday.

"Follow me," commanded the Sergeant.

Crossing the road at breakneck speed, he was soon leading the pair of us down a maze of cobbled streets. His face was blood red, his powerful chest puffed out, his stick no longer tapping the pavement, but whacking it with every stride. With two young policemen being towed along in his wake, he looked majestic. In those mean Ardwick Streets, the word was soon out that he was on the warpath. Front doors opened and young women scuttered out of the two-up, two-downs at the thought of their children being exposed to retribution. As we sailed along the footpath, many of them kept alongside us by running in the roadway, throwing fearful sideways glances at the Sergeant, whilst others overtook us at a sprint and headed towards the school.

Bringing up the rear, was an extremely overweight woman, wearing an overcoat, which she hadn't had time to button. Handicapped by both her weight and an oversized pair of carpet slippers which were slipping off her feet, she flapped and waddled along, losing ground with every stride.

"Save our Errol, warn our Errol," she bellowed continuously to those in front.

Soon she was lost to sight but her voice could still be heard. When we arrived at the school it was a spectacle to behold and only a painting by LS Lowry could have done it justice. The grey playground was bounded on three sides by green, six foot high railings and on the fourth side was the school itself, a Victorian redbrick building with a blue slate roof. On the opposite side of the schoolyard was the playground shelter.

But it was the kids themselves that caught our eye. There were boys everywhere. As our lady informant had quite rightly said, there were hundreds of the little sods. Some were balancing on the railings, some were ripping slates off the shelter roof, windows were being broken and stones flying about. Some boys had even climbed the fall-pipes and were on the school roof. They were everywhere and everyone of them was up to no good. Grouped outside the railings were many of their aproned mothers, each one hollering to her offspring, trying to rescue him (or them), before the storm broke.

Too late! Tom had arrived at the scene and, raising his stick aloft, shouted,

"The bastards, the flaming little bastards!" Feathers ruffled like a turkey cock, he rushed to the school railings, where the anxious mothers redoubled their efforts to encourage their children to escape. It was pure bedlam. "Quick Number Eleven," he shouted to Roy, "get round to the other side of the school. Don't let any of 'em escape." No sooner was Roy dispatched, than Tommy shouted at me, "Ninety-six, watch this side of the railings. Keep it well posted. I'm going in."

With that, he tucked his trousers into his socks, leant his stick against the railings and climbed over. There was instant panic in the playground, as the mothers continued to scream and, with Roy posted on the far side of the railings, the only means of escape was over the school roof. Some 20 boys had realised this and were desperately shinning up the fall-pipes. Tommy had collected his stick and took up the chase. I knew immediately that no arrests were imminent; corporal punishment was to be applied.

Nowadays we see little of it, but on the C Division, in 1949, it was quite acceptable and freely administered. As Tommy raced around the playground he looked fearsome; a powerful wild man in blue uniform. Every time a boy's buttocks came within reach, he landed them one with his stick, shouting, "take that, you little devil". The pursuit went on for a full three minutes and the scene was a mixture of hysteria and hilarity. Children were scattering everywhere, shouting warnings to each other, mothers were yelling and screaming their instructions, Tommy was roaring and Roy and I were laughing in disbelief at the antics being acted out in front of us.

Suddenly, puffing and panting, his face as red as a beetroot, Tommy started chasing one 13-year-old lad the full diagonal length of the playground in my direction. As they neared the railings, he caught the boy with his left-hand and raised him from the ground, preparing to give him a hefty smack across the buttocks with his stick. At this point, the overweight woman in the men's carpet-slippers had floundered up to the railings and was standing by my side. She was breathing heavily but, when she saw what was happening, she found enough breath to gasp:

"Leave him alone you big fat pig, leave him alone, he's mine."

Of all the children milling around in the school playground, Tommy had chosen her Errol to make an example of. Tommy glared at her.

"Don't touch him, Sir. Please don't hit him, Sir."

In seconds, she had elevated Tommy from the sty to the nobility.

"Don't touch him, Sir," she continued, "he's been misled."

"Don't touch him?" bellowed Tommy, "I'll bloody well kill him, missis!" And, with that, he raised the lad until his head was six feet from the ground and he was staring straight down into the Sergeant's purple face. The boy was wearing a grey jersey and grey, below knee-length, short trousers, the fashion in those days, plus long grey socks and black boots. Tommy glared at him. The Ardwick kid had never been so frightened. If 'our Errol' had been named after Errol Flynn, he certainly didn't live up to the image.

At the sound of his mother's voice, his face screwed up into a grimace, "Mam," he sobbed and then, clutching wildly at his groin, he let out a loud gasp, as a stream of hot pee jetted out from under the left leg of his baggy shorts and splashed all over Tommy Alker's barrel chest, followed by a stream of it down the front of his tunic.

"You dirty little devil!" spluttered Tommy in disgust and dropped him forthwith.

A crowd of women standing nearby looked aghast, until one of them cried out,

"He's pissed on the Sergeant. Errol's pissed on the Sergeant."

With that, they all roared with laughter.

There was little else to do but try to salvage a little pride. The Sergeant climbed back over the railings, pulled his trousers out of his socks, adjusted his helmet, smoothed his damp tunic and raised himself to his full height.

"Right-oh, Number Eleven. Right-oh, Ninety-six. That's taught them a lesson they won't forget. That's how we do it!"

And with that he marched us away along the rough streets, to the comparative safety of the main road.

□ □ □ □

It was a few days later that I took my first prisoner. During the late evening, whilst patrolling Hyde Road, close to the Fenians Arch, I heard the sound of breaking glass and saw two men running away from a public house. Instinct told me, correctly as it turned out, that a brick had been thrown through the pub window and that the front runner, the smaller of the two, was the guilty party. I gave chase and within 200 yards, I had caught up with them. The smaller man was now leading his companion by about ten yards. Much to the amazement of the bigger man, I chased past him in pursuit of his mate and caught him a few yards further down the street. I put an armlock on him and marched him back to the pub, passing his colleague on the way. I invited him to join us but, not surprisingly, he declined. In this case of the hare and the tortoise, it was certainly the tortoise's lucky day. The following morning, at the Magistrate's Court, my prisoner pleaded guilty to a charge of malicious damage and was fined for his misdeeds.

A week later and I had taken my second prisoner; a shop-breaker, again during the late evening and on the same stretch of road. Whilst walking along Hyde Road, a pedestrian had seen two men acting suspiciously. He lost sight of them when they disappeared down a passageway which ran behind a row of lockup shops. Soon afterwards, he heard the sound of breaking glass. He quickly found me and I arrived in time to see two men climbing back over the rear gate of a draper's shop, carrying a bag of stolen property. I gave chase, but this time when I caught up with them, I chose to arrest the tortoise in preference to the hare. This one proved rather troublesome, both aggressive and tight-lipped. But, after receiving a good talking to in the DO, he was conned into revealing the name of his accomplice. At the next Quarter Sessions both men received prison sentences.

A Certain Smile – 19 Beat

One often hears the expression, a born policeman and, during my 35 years of service, I certainly met a few of them but they were relatively rare. Policemen are recruited from all walks of life and usually enter the Force as a result of dissatisfaction with their previous employment; only rarely is it to fulfil earlier ambitions. It is from this amalgamation of individuals, each with something different to offer, that the British Police Service draws its humanity, its character, its uniqueness and its strength.

Sadly though, chance can take a man away from his natural habitat and leave him to serve half his lifespan oddly miscast as a policeman, in an environment so different from the one he was reared in, that he finds it difficult to adjust. Such a man was James Stuart.

Jim was a product of the Scottish Highlands, who had come to Manchester to seek employment shortly after the First World War. I first met him in the spring of 1949, when he was an elderly policeman; tall, slim, white haired, with a rather high-pitched voice. He was the officer in charge of the Police Section House at Gorton, a small building situated on Hyde Road, directly opposite the large Belle Vue Gardens. He doted on his daughter and, consequently, she was his favourite topic of conversation. I got to know Jim well in those early days and found that, even after all the years spent in the Manchester area, he had left his heart behind in the Scottish Highlands. He was a congenial person and quite a character, but very erratic and not one I would choose as my mentor. But he was no less a man for that.

After working for six weeks in Ardwick, I moved higher up Hyde Road to 19 Beat, again covering a mainly working class area, with a large estate of council property at its heart, yet considered to be more up market than Ardwick, particularly by the resident Gortonians. Working the beat took me to within a few yards of the section house and I was required to call in as part of my patrol. Jim was always glad to see me, being pleasant, talkative and apparently fond of company.

At 10.45pm on my first night, a Sunday, I walked into the office and placed my cape and lamp on the counter, a sign that I had time to spare. Jim was alone and we talked for a few minutes, mainly and almost inevitably, about his teenage daughter when, quite out of the blue, he asked:

"Have you ever seen a man talk to an owl?"

I looked at him, surprised.

"An owl?"

'Yes," he nodded and smiled excitedly, "it's quite easily done."

I decided he was having me on and pushed my left leg towards him.

"Go on, pull this one, it's got bells on."

"Och, you don't believe me, eh? Well come outside and I'll show ye. I'll see if I can bring an owl down and get it to perch on the yard gate."

Both the Gorton and Levenshulme Section Houses were of the same design; one storey, brick-built and flat-roofed, like the air raid shelters thrown up by the thousand during the Second World War. Each contained a small office, kitchen, storeroom and dining-room which was also used for parades. There was a covered bicycle rack and dog kennels in the small rear yard. To the left hand side of the section house, giving access to the yard, was a six foot high iron gate, opened only when officers were either parading or retiring from duty.

We strolled out into the bright, clear, starlit night with small clouds floating across the face of the moon.

"Perfect!" exclaimed Jim, "simply perfect."

Out there in the yard, he was transformed; a completely different man. Gazing up at the sky, he started hooting like an owl. There is no shortage of owls in the city and, after a short time, Jim made contact. An owl began to circle above us, gradually getting lower, hooting in response to his calls.

"She'll come down and perch on the gate," whispered Jim.

Having listened to the interchange, I no longer doubted that the owl would do just that.

"Stand in the cycle shed, mon," hissed Jim, "and keep ye'sell still and quiet."

In his excitement, his Scot's brogue became more pronounced. I did as I was told. Jim was now hooting very softly, coaxing the bird lower and lower.

"She's here, she's here."

With a soft flurry of wings, the owl landed on the iron gate. From my vantage point, under the roof of the cycle rack, I could see both the owl and Jim, who had concealed himself from the bird's view by standing around the corner of the section house wall. The owl hooted harshly. This time it was Jim who responded, quietly but instantly and the owl cocked its head attentively to one side. Jim peeped around the corner at the bird, then looked across at me with his forefinger to his lips and began hooting again, this time more quietly and insistently, like a baby demanding attention. What followed was, to all intents and purposes, a lengthy discussion, on some unknown subject, between the bird and the elderly Scotsman.

Such rare moments in Manchester are seldom destined to last and we were sharply brought back to reality when the telephone sounded and Jim went inside to answer it; there was urgent business which required my attention. When we finally returned to the yard, the bird had flown.

I had the next night off, so a couple of nights had elapsed before I again had a chance to renew my discussions with Jim. He was alone when I walked into his office at 12.15am but this time he was sitting in front of the gas fire, reading the Manchester Evening News.

"Morning, Jim, how are the owls tonight?"

"Hm, Ninety-six," he replied, absent-mindedly, over the top of the newspaper and returned to his reading without reference to the events of the other night.

I started to pick up my cape and prepared to leave, upon which he immediately put the paper to one side.

"Settle yourself down for a minute," he exclaimed in his high-pitched voice.

He was a man who liked company or, rather, not one who liked to be left on his own. On this occasion he wanted to tell me about the habits of fieldmice. As I listened to him, I realised he was very knowledgeable on the subject but, after a while, I began to lose interest and decided to steer the conversation back to the owls.

"I was telling my parents how you persuaded an owl to land on the gate, Jim. They were amazed."

"Most people are," Jim replied, "it's something I've been doing since I was a wee boy."

In no time at all I had inveigled him out into the backyard and, whilst I crouched in the cycle shed, Jim took up his position in the middle of the yard and began hooting. He had just received his first answering call, when there was a cry from inside the building.

"Excuse me, is there anyone there? Yoo-hoo, anyone there?"

"Damn and blast!" cursed Jim, at the sound of the woman's voice. "Sounds like trouble at this time in the morning."

Entering the office, we assumed our roles as constables once more; he the distinguished white-haired veteran, an authority on all things and me, the boyish, thickset, rosy-cheeked youngster.

In the small office we were confronted by a tiny, agitated, middle-aged woman peering about short-sightedly through a pair of silver-rimmed, pebble glasses. She was wearing a loosely tied floral headsquare and, even though the weather was dry, she was carrying a gent's umbrella.

"You know me. I'm Mrs W from number 5 ... Street," she announced, naming a street which lay about a mile south of the section house. Jim pretended that he knew her, although I don't think he did.

"I've got trouble at home," she continued, "my daughter's taken up with a bad un. She's only fifteen and he's much older than her. They've got themselves locked in my house and they won't let me in. I don't know what they're up to but I know they're in there, that's for sure."

"You're sure they're in there now?" asked Jim.

"Like I say, Sir, I'm certain." Mrs W looked quickly over her shoulder to check if anyone else could overhear, before adding quickly, "I think they're upstairs. I'm sure of it."

"Well," exclaimed Jim, as he slammed his hand down on the desk, "I'll soon sort them out!" His voice rose to an even higher pitch. "Now don't you worry, Mrs W, I'll have you back in your own home in no time at all."

This level of personal involvement surprised me, as most Station Officers would simply have despatched me to deal with the matter. Not Jim. He reached for his helmet and placed it firmly on his head, chinstrap down, in a most determined fashion. It was the first time I had seen him wear it. He shepherded us outside, locked up the station and led us off along Hyde Road at a cracking pace. I began to suspect that the case had serious overtones, at least in Jim's mind.

After a short while, Mrs W began to lag behind. Doing her best to keep up and feeling the need to keep in touch, she began to shout out directions, much to the amusement of the late night pedestrians. I glanced sideways at Jim as I kept up with him. His jaw was jutting out and he looked grim and resolute. Was he associating Mrs W's teenage daughter with his own? If so, heaven help the man she was with!

The quickest route to Mrs W's home lay along the main road but a backwoods man like Jim rarely sticks to the main thoroughfare and it came as no surprise when he suddenly veered off to his left and started to wind his way through the darkened back streets.

"This way, Sir," panted Mrs W, as she pointed along the main road with her over-sized umbrella. To no avail – once Jim had made up his mind, there was simply no holding him back.

Mrs W's voice could still just be heard.

"I'd just been to the second house at the Cozy Cos," she called out at the top of her voice, referring to the Cosmo Cinema. "Then I went for some chips and when I got back at 11 o'clock, I found it all locked up. I've been trying to get in ever since."

With some persuasion, I managed to halt Jim's headlong charge and we waited for her to catch up. But no sooner had she arrived, than he set off again at an even faster rate. The poor woman clutched at my arm, aware that I would soon be obliged to go chasing after my elderly colleague.

"The bad swine's ten years older than her," she gasped frantically. "I know that the police are after him. They've got a warrant out for him."

Jim waited irritably a few yards ahead and, as soon we caught up with him, set off again at a gallop. We finally arrived at a small mid-terraced house and it was here that the situation became confused.

"I'll go round the back," said Jim in a high-pitched stage whisper. "They've probably left the back door open and I'll be able to sneak in quietly." He was soon back with a disappointed look on his face. "Get round the back, Ninety-six, it's all locked up. Wait for me to open the door."

After a few seconds in position, he joined me, stumbling over a metal bucket in the process, making enough noise to waken the dead. "Get back to the front, she's lost her bloody key. I'll have to break in here."

He was itching to begin the assault on the back door and gave me a push to help me on my way. At the front of the house, there was Mrs W, looking sheepish, key in hand.

"I was looking for it in my purse, but it was in my pocket. The other gentleman's got me proper confused."

She wasn't the only one! Clutching my arm, she pointed at the bedroom window.

"Warn the other gentleman to be careful. Him up there's a really nasty swine."

Now that she had got her breath back, she was also speaking in whispers. Goodness knows why, because from the back of the house dull thuds could be heard, as Jim tried to force the back door.

Meanwhile, I had unlocked the front door, forced a small bolt and entered the house. Once inside, the noise from the rear sounded like a small steam hammer. I went through to the kitchen where Jim was bruising himself on a door that was not only locked, but doubly bolted. It would have taken a 22 stone prop forward to have burst through and Jim certainly wasn't one of those. I turned the key in the lock, withdrew the heavy bolts and let him in. He didn't look too pleased, although he must have been grateful. He rushed past me without a word and dashed quickly up the stairs, two at a time. Reaching the top, he literally bounded into the bedroom on the left. A bewildered Mrs W watched, open-mouthed, as he sped past her.

"My goodness me, do be careful, Sir."

Following Jim upstairs at a more sedate pace, I reached the top, as a naked youth ran out of the bedroom on the right. He had meant to run downstairs but, colliding with my shoulder, he was virtually propelled into the other bedroom, where Jim spun round in alarm, thinking that he was about to be attacked. With no such thought in mind, the lad staggered past him and crouched in the far corner of the room, with both hands covering his groin.

We were now in for the biggest surprise of the night, for lying in Mrs W's large double bed, covered with a cotton sheet, were four people! From right to left were Mrs W's heavily-built, 15-year-old daughter, her boyfriend, the much older 'bad un' Mrs W had warned us about, an 18-year-old prostitute named June, whom I had met in my professional capacity a few weeks earlier and her boyfriend for the evening. The youth who was covering his genitals in the far corner of the room, was June's younger brother. We were soon joined by Mrs W, who was almost struck dumb at the sight of a row of strangers in her bed. But as her eyes picked out her daughter from amongst them, she did manage a horrified, "Well I never did!"

Jim had lost much of his composure and, in his high-pitched voice, ordered all four out of the bed.

"Git oot, git oot. D'ya hear?" he bawled in a thick Scottish accent.

From the bed, four pairs of eyes stared at him with a mixture of fright and shock. When there was no sign of movement from any of them, he grasped hold of the bottom of the sheet and started to tug at it furiously.

"Git oot, I tell ye! Git oot, d'ya hear?"

Four pairs of hands clutched the sheet even tighter. At this act of defiance, Jim began to swear loudly and, using all his strength, started heaving away, as if he had entered a tug-of-war contest. The prostitute, still gripping the sheet, found time to smile at me, which infuriated him even more.

"I'll wipe the smile off thee face," he hissed.

Suddenly the battle was won and lost and, when all was revealed, they had only one small vest between the four of them. It also became apparent why the young prostitute could smile – she was wearing it! All five quickly started to dress; four rather sheepishly but June was far more brazen about it, slipping into her knickers and bra as it if was an art form.

Jim decided that we needed assistance and he turned to Mrs W.

"Get ye into Cross Street (a nearby shopping centre). Ye'll find a policeman on duty there. Fetch him here quickly, woman."

As I looked at the motley bunch in the room, I wondered why on earth he needed another policeman. In next to no time Mrs W returned, with not one policeman, but two. They looked inquiringly first at Jim and then at me. Jim looked away and busied himself with chivvying along the young prostitute and I merely shrugged my shoulders. It was getting crowded in the tiny bedroom and one of the older policemen eased the situation by taking the prostitute's brother downstairs. This prompted Jim into escorting Mrs W and the two young women down the stairs and the remaining copper took charge of the prostitute's boyfriend, leaving me with the 'bad un'.

Aware of the warrant out for his arrest and a possible jail sentence to follow, he was more reluctant to be taken into custody than the others. He also seemed annoyed that his pleasures had been so rudely interrupted and, when there were only the two of us left in the bedroom, he became both verbally and physically aggressive. After a bit of bad tempered scuffling, mainly on his part, I picked up his jacket and his boots, pitched them down the stairs and then none too gently bundled him down after them. He was indeed a real nasty devil, with a foul mouth.

Having got him to the bottom of the stairs, I wrestled him into the living-room where the other eight members of the party watched us with interest, as if wondering what all the hostility was about. My prisoner rounded on me, cursing loudly, his fists held high, his eyes blazing. My adrenaline started to flow.

"Hit him!" screamed old Jim at the top of his voice and I promptly slammed a right-hand onto the 'bad un's' chin.

I had never had occasion to strike anyone since my schooldays and I was more than a little surprised, indeed shocked, to see him rocket across the room and land in a crumpled heap on the settee – out like a light.

Aware that what I had done was wrong and completely contrary to my training, I stood there trying to think of a reasonable excuse, should I be required to give one. Then I caught sight of Jim's face; full of pride, eyes sparkling, he was looking at me like a long-lost son. Excuses and secrecy were out of the question. In the next two weeks he was to tell every policeman he met about my one lucky punch, the story becoming more embellished with each telling.

In those days, the Force wasn't as mobile as it is now and with no personal radios to summon transport, we walked our prisoners back to Gorton Section House. Mine was rather subdued by this time and visibly sulking, whilst I was feeling very pleased with myself and ready to share a cheery word with anyone who passed.

On arrival at the section house it was necessary to transfer the prisoners to Divisional Headquarters at Mill Street. Here, in the section house, Jim was in his own domain and there was no doubt as to who was in charge. He scowled at the prisoners as he seated them in the dining-room, mocking the one I had assaulted and making a big performance when requesting the Black Maria – shouting his instructions down the telephone as if we had just arrested a band of dangerous criminals, instead of a bunch of layabouts. After ordering the van, he took time off to feast his eyes on my prisoner's bruised face and then to smile at me approvingly. When the Black Maria arrived, we prepared to load our prisoners. First the two old coppers who had assisted formed an arch, from the section house door to the van, to prevent anyone from escaping – a very professional looking move – and then Jim followed and held the van door open wide. I loaded the prisoners into the van, followed them inside, and then got a nasty shock.

"Charge 'em up, Ninety-six," Jim called in after me.

I turned to face him open mouthed. In response he gave me a knowing wink, flicked his head to one side and looked at me approvingly. He slammed the van door shut and hit the back twice with the flat of his hand as a signal to the driver, who immediately engaged gear and drove off towards Mill Street Station with me, five prisoners, and no senior constable.

The earlier congratulatory glow quickly vanished. I fervently hoped that the man I had arrested really was wanted on warrant and that he had, indeed, engaged in sexual intercourse with a 15-year-old. But what about the other four? What had they done wrong? As for the prostitute, her boyfriend and her brother, I couldn't think of anything and yet here I was, taking them into custody. Was there such a thing as unlawful arrest? I comforted myself with the thought that on the C Division, there probably wasn't.

It was left to the Inspector in the charge office to sort out the complications. Fortunately, the 'bad un' was wanted on warrant and he was placed in the cells. A policewoman was sent for and started to interview the 15-year-old. So far, so good. Now it was the turn of the other three. After a good tongue lashing, he eventually turfed them out of the station and they hurried away, delighted to be free. I stood back, impressed by his technique. When they were well out of earshot, the Inspector then rounded on me and, by the time he had finished, I decided that his attitude towards the prisoners, compared to his verbal assault on me, was downright friendly. I stood to attention in front of him, not knowing what to say except, "Yes, Sir. No, Sir". Tempting though it was in the circumstances, I was beyond the age of blaming others. I felt, and possibly looked, like Stan Laurel when Ollie had landed him in trouble. But it was all part of my education.

Friday Night is Music Night -7 Beat

I'll join the Legion
That's what I will do
And in some far distant region
Where human hearts are staunch and true

Confident of his ability to rouse the fervour of the Ardwick lads, who were packed into the crowded theatre, Josef Locke gesticulated enthusiastically, as he strode to and fro across the stage of the Manchester Hippodrome. As the twin spotlights followed the Irish tenor's movements, I could see, even from the very back of the auditorium, that he was in splendid form. He looked and sounded magnificent. Tall and well-built, attired in evening dress, complete with white, frilled shirt, now open to the waist, bow tie discarded and cast carelessly onto the wooden stage, he strutted about like a peacock. His dark wavy hair was brushed back and glistening with Brilliantine, his moustache bristled and his normally florid complexion was almost purple as he belted it out:

"And so I go to fight a foreign foe, although
I know I'll sometimes be missed
By the girls I kissed."

As if stirred by romantic notions of the Legion and wishing to display the parade ground skills learnt during two years' National Service with the Lancashire Fusiliers, two Ardwick lads left their seats and started to march up and down the centre aisle. Along the back row, some of the less ardent male lovers took time off from their snogging, as thoughts of the Legion held temporary sway over their passions. Behind them, the ice-cream girl stood motionless, her torch shining onto a tray filled with tubs and cornets, as if realising that there was little chance of selling her wares whilst Josef was commanding centre stage. Three or four feet behind her, quite relaxed, stood Sergeant Alker and me. I had adopted my favourite stance, with my left thumb hooked behind the silver button of my breast pocket and leaning lightly back against the theatre wall.

"Good natural voice," commented Tommy Alker, nodding his head towards the stage, "used to be a policeman in Londonderry."

Now it was my turn to nod and look knowledgeable.

"That's right, Sarge. He served less than two years though."

I had had the benefit of interviewing Locke earlier in the week about a practical joke involving two other performers and a dog, the details of which escape me now and it was then that he had told me about his police background.

Suddenly, the Sergeant's attitude altered and he stiffened slightly as he noticed that the two marchers had extended their beat and were now marching directly towards us. Both of military bearing, they were showing off to the girls as, side by side, they kept perfect time to the tinny theatre orchestra. As they approached, the taller of the two spotted the Sergeant and me, smiled broadly and saluted us smartly without losing step. I had taken my thumb from behind my tunic button and was standing erect. Tommy Alker had taken his stick from where it was tucked under his right arm and was leaning on it in a slightly threatening manner. Our faces remained impassive. The message was clear:

"Have fun if you must, but include us at your peril."

The tall lad read it perfectly and called out to his companion:

"Check, TLV off."

With that, they both did a smart about turn and set off towards Josef, who was promising to do his bit and fall for the flag:

"If I must, I'll do or die,

Or know the reason why."

I glanced at my watch; it was 9.40pm. Suddenly there was a slight movement, accompanied by a rustling sound, as a solitary figure appeared through the red plush curtains to the right of Tommy Alker. Even in the semi-darkness, there was no mistaking the outline of Percy, the commissionaire. He sidled up to the Sergeant and even though he lowered his voice to a whisper, I distinctly heard him say, "Compliments of the manager, Sergeant."

Then, sliding sideways, he was by my side, looking directly ahead at he stage but whispering out of the side of his mouth, as if he was arranging something important, yet somewhat illegal.

"Ow are you, kid? Thanks a lot."

With that, he furtively pushed a ten shilling note into my left hand. Obviously another ritual was being performed. I had watched a first-class variety show, whilst being paid police wages for doing so. There had been no suggestion of trouble and I had enjoyed the evening immensely. The generous tip from the theatre management amounted to half a day's pay and I never thought to question why, or how long, the practice had existed. Perhaps it dated back to the days when the music hall could be a violent place.

Seven beat was in Ardwick and its focal point was the Manchester Hippodrome, formerly the Ardwick Empire, occupying, as it did, a prominent position on Ardwick Green. Even now, whenever I think of Ardwick, I remember the dear old Hipp and how lively it was on the Green in the evenings. Although demolished long ago, a sketch of it by Harold Riley hangs on my wall at home.

The shift had started quietly enough at 1.45 that Friday afternoon, as I had paraded for duty at Brunswick Street Section House. I had produced appointments and was patiently waiting, as Sergeant Alker allocated duties to the beat men.

"Ninety-six, Seven Beat. Take late refreshments and then meet me outside the Hippodrome at eight o'clock." He winked and smiled broadly, as if making a joke. "Friday night is music night."

I noticed that some of the older constables were looking at me rather enviously, as if thinking that I was too young in service to enjoy even those perks that existed on my own regular beat. One veteran even let out a sigh of disgust, loud enough for all to hear.

Shortly after parading, I was tied up with a road traffic accident. A young man had been knocked off his cycle and badly injured. I had to accompany him to Manchester Royal Infirmary and so missed my refreshment break. Consequently, I didn't meet up with Sergeant Alker again until the appointed time that evening, but I had gleaned from other constables what was in store for me.

At 7.45 I was standing outside the Hippodrome, exchanging pleasantries with people queueing for admission. I had purposely arrived early, as mingling with the crowds milling around the Green on a Friday night was far more entertaining than patrolling the dismal back streets.

Walking along the queue of people, calling out the price of admission and availability of seats, came Percy, the commissionaire.

"Queueing at ninepence and one shilling, seats at two and ninepence."

We had not been introduced, but I knew him by reputation. Small, chunky and bespectacled, resplendent in green, with massive gold epaulettes and buttons, he looked like Ronnie Corbett in a Zambian Field Marshall's uniform. His goldbraided peaked cap was at least two sizes too big for him and must have had a newspaper or two tucked into the hat band, to stop it slipping down over his eyes. He came to join me and peered jovially into my face, before glancing at the numbers on my collar.

"Ninety-six eh? New lad then. Who's the Sergeant on tonight?"

His accent was pure Ardwick. I was about to answer, when he turned towards Tommy Alker, who had just left the section house and was crossing the cobbles towards us. Percy's eyes lit up.

"Tommy Alker, eh? Great fella, loves the show," before adding, unnecessarily, "Josef Locke's on tonight, packs 'em in, that fella does," and then confiding, "he's always half pissed you know."

Drunk or sober, Josef was certainly at his best that evening and the two hours at the Hipp passed only too quickly.

Without doubt, the Palace Theatre on Oxford Street was the grander of the two theatres and usually boasted more international artistes on its bill, but the Hipp captivated the spirit of the British music hall. It was a rollicking place; gay, colourful, loud, more than a little risqué and, especially if Frank Randle was on the bill, downright vulgar.

At five to ten, Tommy Alker nudged me none too gently.

"Come on, young man, time to retire. Percy seen you alright?"

I held the ten shilling note in my pocket and nodded.

"Night, Sarge, night, Ninety-six." Percy saluted us smartly as we left the foyer and then called me back. "Quick word, Ninety-six, if you please." He glanced at me owlishly over the top of his horn-rimmed spectacles. "If ever you want to bring your wife, or girlfriend, along on a Tuesday or Wednesday, you'll both be more than welcome as guests of the establishment. Freebies you know."

As I lived several miles away, was not married and had no regular girlfriend at that time, I never took him up on his offer. However, many policemen did, some taking both their wives and girlfriends along, but obviously on different nights!

Over the years I have seen great changes in the Police Service, not all of them for the better. Nowadays, each Force will have a department solely concerned with community contact and great store is set by the mutual interchange between police and public. In earlier days, such arrangements were unnecessary, as the vast majority of Police Officers were in direct daily contact with the community. I believe that it is an indication of failure, on the part of the police, that they are now deemed necessary. Somewhere between the two periods, we have lost our way, and young policemen no longer understand the true meaning of beatwork.

When there were no traffic wardens, or school crossing patrols, the tasks of regulating the flow of traffic and the safety of the children were part of the daily duties of the beat policeman. The benefits gained were enormous and children grew up with far more respect for the police than is evident today. Children knew the policeman they saw every day journeying to and from school. Of course, he changed duties from time to time, so that eventually they came to know several policemen by sight and whilst they may have had their favourites, each commanded the same authority. More importantly, the children thought that the individual policemen knew each and every one of them, which made their supervision that much easier! Not only did the police oversee their journeys to and from school and share in their achievements, but they were also in attendance when the children's matinees finished at the main road cinemas.

In another prominent position on Ardwick Green, standing opposite the Hippodrome, was the large, modern Apollo Cinema. Opened by Margaret Lockwood in 1938, it had a seating capacity of 2800. It was an experience on a Saturday lunchtime to be present when the doors were flung open and around 2000 excited children swarmed out in a massive, heaving, cheering throng.

There was never any need to ask what the main feature had been. If it had been a science fiction film, all the budding Dan Dares would rocket off along the pavement, emitting sounds similar to police sirens. The youngsters were even more adroit at imitating their cowboy heroes. Gangs of boys would push through the cinema doors, form into posses, then, with left hand tucked under the chin, they would rein in an imaginary horse, rocking back on their heels as they did so and vigorously slapping their backsides. As they raced along, they acted as outriders to the trams, occasionally letting off a volley of shots in the direction of the tram driver. Should he return their fire with extended fore and middle fingers, as many did, another dozen or so kids would appear and join in the ambush.

Knowing the children from such an early age, it was rare that they would wish to assault you in later years.

Close to another corner of Ardwick Green, was Brunswick Street Section House, an end-terrace with a chequered history. Built a century or so earlier, as a 'fine dwelling, it had more recently been used as a common lodging-house, a brothel and an auxiliary fire station during the early war years, before finally ending up in police hands. In the cellar was kept the coal to fuel the kitchen fire and, by 1949, a sack of sugar had also found its way there. Occupying the ground floor was the front office, the dining-room, the kitchen and the scullery. On the first floor, only the parade room and the bathroom and toilet were in use, whilst the other rooms and attics had fallen into neglect. Of the division's three section houses, it was the busiest by far and quite possibly the busiest in the city. It was manned by a Station Officer, assisted by the Station Beatman and Patrolman, who spent most of their duty time either inside, or within close proximity to the station.

On one side, our neighbour was Nurse Duckworth, a jovial middle-aged Irish district nurse, who was forever running short of rationed goods. At any hour of the day, she was likely to enter the front office, carrying a large cream-coloured milk jug. "Be Jesus, I'm out of milk again!" or asking whether there was any tea or sugar to spare. Milk was always available at Brunswick Street Station. It was delivered daily by one dairy and collected from another. Money never changed hands. The empty bottles were kept in the scullery and when that room was full, a milk float would come and remove them. The request for a milk float was generally prompted by an expected visit from the Superintendent, who once flew into a rage at the sight of 180 empty milk bottles, standing to attention in rows of three.

There was no canteen and we cooked our own food in the kitchen. A brew (tea and sugar) for four people, was supplied by the Force canteen at a charge of three ha'pence – about half a penny in decimal currency. Milk was, of course, free.

In return for our milk, tea or sugar, the jolly, rotund Nurse Duckworth not only provided expert first aid treatment when required, but also put up with quite a lot of disturbance, particularly in the early hours of the morning, when a violent prisoner was being given the rounds of the kitchen. This would always prompt an early call from her next morning, jug in hand,

"Be Jesus, you kept himself (Mr Duckworth) up half the night with the shinnanikins."

On the other side of the section house was Hope Hall, whose elderly, gentle minister left us well alone, preferring to attend to the spiritual needs of those in the streets close by.

☐ ☐ ☐ ☐

"Ah, Ninety-six, bang on time. I like to see a youngster who's punctual and interested in the job."

Passing along Ardwick Green, I had called into the station to see if there were any jobs needing my attention. Standing by the counter, I looked quizzically at Sandy, the veteran Station Officer, puzzled by the unusually fussy greeting. Nearing the end of his service, Sandy was an excellent Police Officer who, although not in good health, rarely took time off work and had been entrusted with this, the busiest of police stations. He was not, however, renowned for his patience, nor for extending sympathy to probationers such as myself. Along with other young constables, I had often felt the sharp end of his tongue and this was the first time he had exchanged pleasantries with me.

"How are you getting on?" he enquired, in his softest Scottish brogue.

"Fine thanks, Sandy."

I decided to chance my arm and call him Sandy for the first time. He positively beamed at me.

"You live in Stockport, don't you?" It was more of a statement than a question. I nodded, wondering how he knew. "Hilly town," he added, conversationally, "too hilly for me, with my bronchial trouble." He let out a wheezing cough, as if to demonstrate his complaint, eyeing me all the time in a fatherly fashion. "Long way to travel home. Do you cycle it?"

"No, only early on Sunday mornings when there's no public transport running, otherwise I use the bus or the tram."

"It's a long way all the same," he continued, casually, "today I may be able to do you a good turn."

I was immediately on my guard. Although an outstanding policeman and a very nice man, he never went out of his way to do good turns for anyone of my lowly status. He read the look in my eyes perfectly and hastened to allay my fears.

"Aye," he confided even more softly than before, "I've got a found dog in the back. It's only a little puppy and it needs taking up to Levenshulme."

Now I was beginning to understand. Here at Brunswick Street there was no accommodation for found dogs. The puppy would have to be

56

transferred to Levenshulme Section House which had been purpose-built with the necessary kennels. As there was no police transport on the division, I was expected to deliver the puppy by bus. Sandy leant across the counter, obviously about to offer me an inducement.

"If you come back at nine o'clock, I'll sign you off duty. You can take the puppy to Levenshulme and retire there. It'll guarantee you an early finish and put you two miles nearer home."

It was certainly a worthwhile inducement and one I would be foolish to refuse. I glanced at the large round clock on the wall – it was 7.30.

"I'll call in at nine thirty," I replied, rather conscientiously, "it'll take me half an hour at the most on the bus."

But old Sandy would have none of this.

"No, you've got to look after number one in this job," he pronounced, with authority. "You come in here at nine o'clock and I'll sign you off."

So I left the station and worked my beat for the next hour and a half, with the pleasant feeling that I was now accepted, even by the old ones.

At 9pm I presented myself at the counter.

"Ah, Ninety-six. Come on now. I've got them tied up in the back."

"Them? I thought it was one small puppy."

"Yes, it was, but I've had another two brought in since then."

Still very pally towards me, he led me into the kitchen, where it was immediately obvious that I had been conned. Sitting on the brown linoleum, in front of the large open fire, were two of the scruffiest dogs imaginable. Close to them, with his back to the fire, was an equally scruffy male puppy, who was being sexually active with a tall, three-legged stool. But it was the largest of the dogs which grabbed my attention. The size of a small donkey, it sensed that I had come to remove it from its privileged fireside position and it rolled back its lips to reveal a set of enormous yellow molars. As I stared at those teeth, the lips moved menacingly, as if being plucked by invisible fingers.

"He's very docile," Sandy reassured me. "Speak to him gently and he responds quite well."

I observed that Sandy had tied a piece of string around each of the animals' necks, the ends of which he had cunningly plaited to form a single lead. Seizing the plaited string and unwinding it from the cellar doorknob, he hoisted the dogs to their feet, disengaged the puppy from its stool and escorted us swiftly along the corridor to the front door. Pushing three Found Property reports into my tunic pocket and wrapping the plaited string around my wrist, he almost ejected me from the station.

"You could be in Stockport well before ten o' clock. Time for a pint before they close," he called after me.

Crossing a crowded Ardwick Green, the over-sexed puppy was up to his tricks again. Ignoring the donkey-sized dog, he was concentrating his affections on the third of the trio, a small, mangy, brown and white mongrel, who was forced to scurry along with his tail tucked between his legs and his backside brushing the cobbles. I increased the puppy's difficulties by dragging the three of them along at breakneck speed, forcing him to chase the others on his hind legs, like a circus performer.

At the bus stop, outside the Apollo Cinema, I joined a group of people on the footpath. To give the other dogs a bit of peace and to save myself further embarrassment, I pushed the puppy into a sitting position and trapped his tail between my boot and the pavement.

"I think you've got your foot on the dog's tail, Officer," observed the man standing next to me.

"Yes, and that's where it's staying until the bus comes." I snapped, without further explanation.

Fortunately, a bus arrived within minutes.

There's no knack in getting three such dogs onto the top deck of a bus other than determination. I had a quick word with the driver then, grabbing the puppy by the scruff of the neck, I manhandled the other two up the narrow twisting staircase. Once upstairs, I gratefully flopped onto the back seat with helmet askew and yanked the three dogs towards me. I looked up to find that every passenger on the top deck had turned round to stare at us and, on cue, the puppy became romantically attached to my right leg. At this, old yellow fangs, who was almost sitting on my lap, flattened his lips across his enormous teeth and slavered on me, as if attempting to join in the joke.

During the journey, the puppy kept up his performance, lavishing his charm on everything within range – my leg, the other dogs, the seats, prancing along the entire gangway on its hind legs, its backside moving about like a fiddler's elbow. Having arranged with the driver to make an unscheduled stop at Levenshulme Section House, I was more than a little relieved to see the familiar blue sign. Luckily, the dogs were as eager as I was to get off the bus and raced along the pavement to where Paddy, the Station Officer, was waiting to put them into the kennels. I followed him into the office and handed him the report forms. Whilst he reached for the dog register, I glanced at the clock, it was twenty past nine.

"Right now, Ninety-six," he tutted, "Sandy says you're to have an early finish." He looked at me and shook his head disapprovingly. "Early finish indeed and you with your number hardly dry! It never happened to me when I had only your service in. You youngsters don't know you're born."

I thought that perhaps he was joking but it was clear that he was annoyed at the extra work I was causing him, so near to his finishing time.

"Well don't worry yourself about it, Paddy," I replied testily, "I'm damned sure I wont be volunteering for any more."

☐ ☐ ☐ ☐

My first encounter with death came a few days later. Many of the older policemen hated dealing with deaths but not for reasons of compassion or squeamishness but because a coroner's report had to be made out. My first encounter came about when an elderly lady was knocked down by a heavy lorry and fatally injured, only 50 yards or so from where I was escorting schoolchildren across Hyde Road. There was a screech of brakes and I saw what appeared to be a bundle of rags rolling down the road. It was immediately apparent that there was little I could do. In the ambulance, on the way to Manchester Royal Infirmary, I held the old lady's hand and sought to comfort her, but she died on the way.

In those days, on the C Division, probationary constables were not allowed to submit fatal traffic accident reports and a very capable Irish Sergeant was placed in charge of the incident. I helped him to make an inventory of the old lady's possessions which was a sad duty. Bundles of letters dating back 70 years and tied in blue ribbon, cases of scissors and needles and samples of embroidery work, all had to be listed, along with her other worldly possessions. I was impressed by the way the Sergeant conducted the enquiry and particularly his penmanship – he covered every aspect of the case sympathetically. I was soon to discover another facet to his character and found that 90% of his time was spent with both feet firmly planted in mid-air.

Funny Walks – 23 Beat

The scholars' walk in Manchester
Is quite a pretty sight,
The boys all have their faces washed,
Their boots with blacking bright,
The girls all have their hair in curl,
Their dresses spotless white.

Roger Oldham, *Manchester Alphabet*

Twenty-three Beat covered the working-class district of West Gorton and it was here that I had my first experience of the Whit Week Walks and again met one of the most delightful and unusual characters it has been my pleasure to meet.

When Mancunians speak of the Whit Week Walks they are either referring to the joint Anglican Church procession, which took place on Whit Monday, or the joint Roman Catholic Church procession, on Whit Friday. On both occasions, Manchester city centre was closed to traffic, in order to accommodate both the parade and the spectators.

The very first procession was held in 1801 and was an immediate success. The following is a description of the centenary procession which took place in 1901:

"The scene in Albert Square this morning was one of exceptional beauty. At eight o'clock the space in the square was so arranged by the marshals ,that the place of each school was indicated by a flag flying the Union Jack ... Then, for the next half hour, the different schools arrived in quick succession and the music from a dozen bands proceeded from the square.

There was a free mingling of colour, the cassocks and hoods of the clergy contrasting sharply with the costumes worn by the scholars ... The Chetham boys, wearing the quaint garments of the school order, formed a prominent feature. Nathaniel Dumville ... unfurled his white flag to act as a baton and, to the beating of his time, nearly 30,000 young voices sang the Old Hundredth. The schools marched out of the square, the order being determined by the date of consecration of their respective churches. At every point on the route were gathered large crowds of sightseers."

Having been a close observer of the walks over a number of years, I find the above description rather too rosy and one which leaves the reader with a false impression. True, it is an accurate account of events when the weather was perfect. But all too often, in Manchester, the Whitsuntide weather is foul and then, the sight of thousands of young, scantily-clad children being herded through the streets in driving rain was very depressing. The bitterness of the rival factions, which all too often erupted into drunken brawling, left me feeling that many of the organisers were more concerned with their own brand of religion, than they were with Christianity.

The walks which gave me the most pleasure, were those held on Whit Sunday, by the local individual churches. The beat bobby was directly involved with them, because he not only escorted the procession around the parish, but became an essential part of the parade. I found all the local walks enjoyable but, as so often is the case, it was the first one which was the most memorable, though for less than obvious reasons.

On my first Whit Sunday on the C Division, I was instructed to parade at 1 pm, an hour earlier than usual, at Gorton Section House, dressed in best day uniform. In those days, this consisted of a closed-neck tunic, helmet with chin-strap down and white cotton gloves, either carried or worn. As I entered the police station, Jim, the white-haired Station Officer, was pushing a huge dog reluctantly towards the kennels. It didn't want to move its feet and I could see that Jim's determined pushing, was causing the great silly thing to fold up like a concertina. Seeing me in my dress uniform, Jim decided not to ask for help; the dog was shedding hair all over the place.

"My God, you look like a new tanner in a sweep's earhole," he grunted, as he heaved the Gorton St Bernhard through the back door. "Sergeant's waiting for you in the parade room."

Entering the small parade room, I found I was very much the junior member of a team of three, detailed to escort one of the larger processions, organised by St Mark's Church, which was situated in Clowes Street, West Gorton. One of the other two team members was Paddy, the Section Sergeant who had dealt so competently with the fatal accident report. The other team member was Tom, a senior constable.

The Sergeant was an ex-guardsman who, although nearing the end of his Police Service, carried himself in a smart military manner and was always immaculately turned out. He was a lovable Irishman, six foot tall, slim but wiry, with dark hair a rosy complexion and high cheek bones. He was an excellent penman, who had a good working knowledge of the law. He could have risen above his present rank but for one small fault, in common with the stage image of an Irishman, he neither could, nor would, allow work to interfere with his drinking, which was a pity.

Years earlier, he had been transferred to C Division from A Division. His behaviour in the city centre was found not to be in keeping with the highest traditions of the Police Service. Well into daylight hours he had been found drunk and fast asleep in a gutter. So, for him, C Division was the end of the line; there was nowhere else for him to go. Not since before the war had anyone been either demoted, or sacked, on the division and he quickly settled in and continued to enjoy life, living it to the full.

As in the Armed Services, Sergeants are the backbone of the Police Service and when I was a young bobby they were, generally speaking, a staunch lot. Paddy, although possibly a little misguided, was such a Sergeant. Today, however, when complaints against the police are numerous and usually thoroughly investigated, he would not be tolerated, despite his many good points.

On my arrival at Gorton Section House, I was impressed by his appearance and obvious keenness. Apart from assisting him briefly with the fatal accident report, this was the first time that I had worked with him and was amazed at his impatience to get things moving. As the Station Officer had pointed out, he was anxiously waiting for me to arrive, even though I was 20 minutes early.

There was no formal parade, no production of appointments, no read up, no list of stolen vehicles to look for; he simply picked up his stick and hastily donned his helmet.

"Come on, Tom, come on Ninety-six. Let's get down to St Marks."

That's what I think he said but I was never quite sure because, apart from his accent, which didn't help, he possessed the most ill-fitting set of false teeth I'd ever come across. As he spoke, the top set took on a life of its own. So, to prevent it rattling about, he would jam it into place with the stub of a pencil, which he carried for the purpose.

After giving us our brief instructions, he gave a wide smile come semi-yawn, settled his teeth back into position, placed the pencil stub back into his pocket and led us briskly out into the streets. As we marched side by side, there was an eagerness in his step which I couldn't understand. I glanced at my watch, it was not yet 12.45. The church was little more than a mile away and the procession wasn't due to start until two. I matched him stride for stride.

"We're setting off early, Sarge," I commented.

I couldn't make any sense of his reply but I could detect a sense of urgency in his tone and noted that he maintained his speed. As we neared the church, the crowds became denser and we were forced to reduce speed and, on occasions, walk in the roadway. The atmosphere in Clowes Street was electric but as Paddy's presence became known and he started to mingle with the crowd, it became less charged and more jovial. In this district he was not only popular, but loved by the local people and he either smiled, nodded, or spoke, to everyone he met.

As I had predicted, we were far too early and the procession had barely started to form. From every angle, mothers were converging on the scene with their beautifully dressed children. The drab street was beginning to take on a new life. I glanced up at the sky – it was cloudless. Standing next to Paddy, the centre of so much attention, I was soon basking in the carnival atmosphere and his reflected glory.

A few yards down the street the bandsmen were tuning their instruments. Close by, the mothers of West Gorton were wiping noses, retying hair ribbons, straightening hats and caps, pulling up socks, scolding the notoriously untidy and using the now grubby handkerchief to give a last rub to new shoes. The Sunday School teachers, all dressed in their finery, were sorting out the pink ribbon which, when held by the smaller children, helped to keep them in position. I found myself surrounded by this mass of women and children; neighbourly groups of mothers, grandmothers, aunts, older sisters, all nicely turned out for the occasion but hardly any sign of their menfolk. It only took seconds to find out where they were.

"Just time for a quick one," said the Sergeant. "Follow me."

Dealing good naturedly with a lot of banter from the elderly women when they saw the direction he was taking, he eased his way through the crowd and straight into the front door of a pub opposite the church. All eyes centred on us as a hush fell over the crowded smoke-filled room and we heard the occasional whisper – "the law!" Paddy's smile encompassed everyone – churchgoer and villain alike. He called out a greeting to the landlord, placed his order by raising three fingers in the air and pushed his way through to the kitchen, where the landlord's three children screamed out in delight.

"Uncle Paddy's come, Uncle Paddy's come."

Such was his effect upon them, that the youngest, a little girl of about five, rushed out into the bar shouting excitedly.

"Daddy, Daddy, Uncle Paddy's come and he's got two other policemen with him!"

I felt my neck turning scarlet under my tight tunic collar. We sat down close to the table on three hard-backed chairs, soon to be joined by the landlord's beaming wife, who entered the kitchen carrying a tray on which there were three pints of newly-drawn black and tan. For the information of the non-drinking reader, in those days a pint of black and tan consisted of half a pint of Draught Guinness, mixed with half a pint of Chester's Fighting Ale – potent stuff indeed. The Sergeant loosened all the hooks and eyes on his tunic collar, placed his helmet close to the table and smiling benevolently at the children, settled himself down. Sensing that he was preparing for a long stay, I became alarmed. As a probationary constable, I was in no position to advise him or, indeed, express my displeasure. I felt trapped.

In an effort to convey to him that there was duty to be done, I made the mistake of drinking my pint of black and tan quickly and then looking from him to the senior constable, in an attempt to convey that we were due to depart. Paddy, being such a decent fellow, misinterpreted my body language. With a look of amused approval on his face, he raised himself from his seat, crossed to the kitchen door, raised three fingers aloft and called across the hubbub to the landlord.

"Get 'em in again, Arthur, the young Officer's thirsty."

I was even more mortified when, a short time later, he repeated the order! With two pints of black and tan already under my belt, I was feeling decidedly anxious about the procession, which I was sure must have formed up, ready to move on. I toyed with my third pint. It was good ale but circumstances were preventing me from enjoying it. Nevertheless, the alcohol gave me enough courage to suggest, as casually as I could, that perhaps we should be making a move.

"Don't worry, Ninety-six, you'll hear the band when they're organised, they won't be ready yet."

The senior constable came to the rescue.

"We should be off by now, Sarge. We'll take the procession round, then come back for a few more at our leisure."

That was obviously the way to do it and certainly had more effect than all my panicking. In order to remove any remaining obstacle, I picked up my beer and gulped it down.

The Sergeant was impressed and, with the help of his pencil stub, called over to the landlady.

"Did you see that? The young un's got a good drop on him."

I then made the first of two mistakes. I showed my complete inexperience by leaving the pub without first going to the lavatory. The second mistake was made when, in my impatience to get started, I led the other two outside. As I stood in the pub doorway, allowing my eyes to become accustomed to the bright sunlight, I was shocked to find that the procession had long since formed up and every eye in West Gorton was fixed upon me, having patiently waited for the police to put in an appearance.

In the middle of the roadway, opposite the pub door, stood the vicar, dressed in his white surplice and obviously very anxiously biding his time. He was ready to move off, but he couldn't proceed without us and neither could he bring himself to enter the pub and disturb us. As I emerged, he proved to me what a good man he was. Whilst the crowd cheered good-naturedly, his face lit up in a wide beaming smile. He then raised his hand high and waved it as a signal to the bandmaster. The band struck up, *Anchors A Weigh*, and the procession finally started to move off down Clowes Street.

The speed of events caught the Sergeant by surprise, leaving no time for perfect diction. He caught me by the shoulder, pointed with his stick down Clowes Street to where the band was marching and rattled his teeth in my right ear. I understood perfectly. I was to lead the parade. Knowing the form, the senior constable was already walking to the back of the procession. Paddy and the vicar were to control the middle section.

I pulled on my white gloves, raced along the procession, speedily overtook the band and placed myself at the head of the walk. Here, well away from the pub and all those staring eyes, I felt very proud. I set my pace to the tempo of the music and, on occasions, turned round and marched backwards as I had seen in films.

"Good stuff this," I thought.

After about a hundred yards, I was horrified when I realised that no instructions had been given as to the route we were to follow. On parade in the Section House, the Sergeant had simply told me to follow him. Confident that the bandmaster would know the way and aware that no motorist had ever run over the Co-op band, I allowed myself to drop back and walk behind them.

My new position was to the offside of the first party of children, the very young ones, who were being led down the centre of the road at a sedate pace. Strolling next to me, her hips swaying gently in time to the music, was one of the Sunday school teachers; a lovely-looking girl about my own age and I stupidly thought that my luck was in. She was tall and slender and her long fair hair flowed down her back. Wearing an ankle length blue dress and a small blue hat entwined with forget-me-nots, she carried a posy of spring flowers in her left hand and a silver-painted shepherdess's crook in her right. Possibly she was feeling self-conscious in this outfit, and this had affected her attitude but I was soon made to realise that a 20-year-old probationary Police Constable, smelling strongly of beer, was not considered eligible when, in a clumsy attempt to compliment her, I told her that she looked like Little Bo-Peep. She scowled at me under her long eyelashes. She was not amused and, in a manner not really becoming of a Sunday school teacher, she told me so. For the next mile or so, at every opportunity, she continued to give me earache.

By this time, Bo-Peep was the least of my worries. The three pints of black and tan had now reached my bladder and I realised that I desperately needed to find a lavatory. We were making a circular tour of the parish, if that's how one can describe walking round a square, moving in an anti-clockwise direction and now heading back towards the church. My need was becoming urgent and my walking was badly affected. The only public toilet was way ahead. If I maintained the pace the young children were setting, I would never make it in time. When the toilet came into sight, I almost fell over my feet in the rush to relieve myself.

On rejoining the procession, the long, hard, utterly-disgusted-with-you glare from Bo, was more than enough to deflate my self-importance and, on seeing the church in the distance, I positioned myself next to the bandmaster, a much older and more tolerant person!

Back at the church, the Sergeant was in his element. He complimented the parents, had a word with the children, shook hands warmly with the vicar and then went to wish goodbye to the Sunday school teachers, who were gathered by the church gate. He behaved like a member of the royal family! As he approached Bo-Peep, I positioned myself discreetly behind him. Surely she must have guessed that he was responsible for my condition and, like him though I did, I was hoping that he was about to get his just deserts. But did he? On the contrary. After complimenting her, she smiled up at him sweetly, almost coyly in fact. "Thank you, Sergeant. How nice to see you again."

She pretended I wasn't there! So much for young women.

As we walked away I asked him what was his secret with the ladies. He looked at me oddly, then jammed the pencil stub up against his top set and said, (I think)

"Personal magnetism."

Turning a Blind Eye – 4 Beat

Rows of small sombre houses with their numbers, door knockers and letterboxes brightly picked out in silver paint and splashes of silver paint spattered on doors and steps, let you know that you were on 4 Beat. This impoverished area stretched from Ardwick Green to Piccadilly Station (London Road, as it was called in those days), then it extended eastwards to Great Ancoats Street.

Under one of the long line of railway arches, which ran the full diagonal length of the beat, slept Peter the Painter. During the day, his stooped figure could often be seen wandering around the district. He was easily recognised by his shuffling gait, battered trilby hat, paint-stained clothes and the two small brushes sticking out of the breast pocket of his tattered jacket. He charged the housewives of Ardwick sixpence to paint the numbers on their front door, or a shilling for the door knocker, or letterbox. A few would give him two shillings just to get rid of him.

He was an articulate and well-educated man but few people ever stayed long enough in his company to discover why he was now a vagrant. At night, under the railway arch, it was possible to detect his presence just by sniffing the air. His coating of dirt and grime made it difficult to put an age to him – perhaps he was 60, maybe more. He slept and prepared scraps of food amidst a litter of bricks and scrap metal in a corner of the arch. He was not a well man and it was a mystery how he survived the bitter winters, huddled miserably over a small fire.

He was always polite and when he approached a house to solicit trade, or to scrounge an early morning cup of tea, as soon as the front door was opened in response to his knock, Peter would raise his battered trilby, with silver-stained fingers.

"Good morning, Madam. Would you care to have your door numbers or door knocker refurbished?"

"You what?"

"Your door numbers, or knocker, or indeed your letterbox, Madam. Would you care for me to repaint them for you?" he persisted, again touching his trilby.

"Not this morning, thank you."

"But, Madam, it will certainly improve the appearance of your front entrance and there's no one who would do it more cheaply – sixpence for up to three numbers."

"Sorry, I've not got time this morning. I've got to get the kids off to school."

"But, Madam, you can trust me. Pay me now and I will guarantee to finish the job whilst you attend to your duties."

"No thanks."

"But, Madam … "

"Look, Peter, shove off will yer. There'll only be trouble with my husband if I let you touch the door."

"Certainly, Madam. I've no wish to either annoy you, or cause you any tribulation. Perhaps you could offer me a cup of tea. My tea-making facilities have let me down this morning."

"Alright, then. On the step mind you."

Again, the trilby would be raised.

"Certainly, Madam, on the step would do perfectly. I've my own supply of sugar."

One summer's afternoon he had wandered down Stockport Road and was canvassing trade along a nice avenue of houses in Levenshulme where he was virtually unknown. An irate householder wanted me to arrest him for contravening the Vagrancy Act. Unfortunately, when Peter was arrested, you had to fumigate him, the prison van, the cell and finally yourself and it was far easier to order him back to his railway arch.

Fortunately, the powers given to British Police Officers are arbitrary and sometimes a policeman will utilise this discretion to his own advantage, or if he feels an offender should be treated leniently. An arrest could often offend a Senior Officer, usually the Charge Office Inspector. This happened to me once, when I was working on 4 Beat.

It was early afternoon on a hot summer's day and I was making my way along Ardwick Green, at the regulation pace of two and a half miles per hour, a pace one quickly adopted. About a quarter of a mile away, I could see an elderly lady making her way across the busy road and, even at that distance, I could see that she was ill and distraught, as she struggled with a battered brown suitcase, half carrying it and half dragging it along behind her. She appeared to have used up all her strength and energy by the time she had reached the steps of the Manchester Hippodrome, where she flopped down wearily, opened a brown paper carrier bag and started to throw small pieces of bread to the pigeons which had gathered round her feet. As if even this small act of kindness was too much for her, she suddenly slumped forward, whilst still maintaining her sitting position and then, somehow, managed to find the strength to steady herself, before finally lolling sideways across the steps. I hastened to her assistance and found that she appeared to be in a coma. I knelt down by her side, held her by one hand and gently shook her by the shoulder whilst asking softly if she was alright.

She listlessly opened one eye and struggled to focus it on me. It looked as if it was all up with her and I was contemplating calling for an ambulance when her lips contorted into a sneer.

"Fuck off," she hissed between clenched teeth.

I was still young and inexperienced enough to be astonished at such coarse language from an elderly lady and stupidly encouraged a repeat performance by saying:

"I beg your pardon?"

"You," she hissed again, "fuck off and leave me alone."

I had never heard a woman curse as this one did. Then I detected the smell on her breath – meths.

I later discovered that she had spent most of the lunchtime in one of the local pubs, drinking a mixture of their beer and her own methylated spirits, until she had finally been ejected by the landlord.

"She made the toilet stink worse than a tiger's cage," he later told me.

I was concerned that she either could not, or would not, stand up and, as such, was committing one of the commonest of offences – D and I – drunk and incapable whilst in a public place.

"I'm taking you in," I told her.

Sprawled as she was on the steps of the Manchester Hippodrome, I didn't consider that I had much option. I hoisted her to her feet, picked up the battered suitcase and, crossing Ardwick Green, managed to get her into Brunswick Street Station, less than 100 yards away. She made a dramatic entrance, for once inside she promptly collapsed across the office counter with her head and arms dangling over the counter top like a rag doll. Sandy, the veteran Station Officer, crossed the room, put one hand under her chin and forced her to look at him.

"Hello, Sylvia," he said, "been at the meths again?"

She attempted a grin.

"Hello, Sandy. No, I've not. It's the young git here. He wanted a bit of how's your father and he's brought me in 'cos I refused him."

Sandy nodded.

"Have you pissed yourself, Sylvia?"

"Aye, I have indeed, Sandy." She tried unsuccessfully to imitate his Scottish brogue, "would you care to check?"

"Not now, Sylvia." Sandy looked at me as if I should have known better. "Take her through to the kitchen, Ninety-six and let her lie on the floor. Don't let her sit down anywhere."

After carrying out his instructions, I returned to the office, where Sandy sadly shook his head at me.

"Send for the van," he sighed, "but you won't be welcome at Mill Street."

"I can take her out and lose her," I suggested, but Sandy wouldn't hear of it and shook his head.

"Once you've locked someone up, they stay locked up."

It was sound advice. Although an officer was allowed discretionary powers, he had to be decisive. Once he had decided on a course of action, it was best for him to stick to it. Releasing prisoners unnecessarily could, quite often, lead to suggestions of unlawful arrest, or similar complaints at a later date.

When the Black Maria arrived, I took her to Mill Street Headquarters, where I cautioned her and charged her with the offence. The reserve man then set about the task of cleaning her up before he could place her in the cells. In the confined space of the warm charge office, she smelt like a yard full of tomcats.

As Sandy had predicted, we were not well received and, as I was leaving the station, the Inspector turned to the clerk and said in a loud voice:

"I don't know who's the bigger pigging nuisance, him or her."

The next morning, Sylvia, an old prostitute, appeared before the magistrates. It was her 274th appearance and she was fined £2 and given time to pay.

But she hadn't finished with me yet. As we left the court together, we entered Minshull Street and I was about to bid her, Good morning, when she abruptly quit the footpath and sauntered into the roadway, directly in front of a slow-moving lorry. Dropping the battered suitcase immediately in front of the nearside front wheel, she forced the driver to stop. He leaned out of his cab, an astonished expression on his face.

"Where you going to, cock?" screeched Sylvia.

"Liverpool."

"That'll do."

With that, Sylvia retrieved the suitcase, opened the nearside cab door, threw the case in, climbed in after it and sat beside the driver. When he turned to look at me, I was already disappearing inside the courthouse, not to venture out again until I was sure she had definitely gone. How the Liverpool police handled her would be their business.

An occasion when I exercised the same discretionary powers to suit my own convenience occurred almost at the same time and close to the same spot on 4 Beat. As a newcomer to the C Division, I had been offered either April or October for my summer leave and had picked October. 1 had also arranged a day out in Blackpool on one of my rest days, with my current girlfriend. We were to take the Ribble bus from Manchester and intended to go on a Thursday, quite early in the morning, to give us a full day there. At that time I was on the 2pm – 10pm relief, the weather was fine and the forecast for the rest of the week was excellent.

On the Wednesday before our proposed day out, I was walking along Higher Ardwick, towards the Green, when a trolley bus slowed down to a crawl and, as it approached, the driver leant out of the window to make a complaint. He jerked his thumb behind him and said,

"Better get down to Ardwick Green, Officer, there's a right bloody comedian arsing about in the middle of the road. Bound to get knocked down unless somebody sorts him out."

Increasing my speed, I made my way towards the Green and found a well-dressed, middle-aged man, doing a balancing act along the tram tracks. Much to the annoyance of the motorists and the amusement of the pedestrians, he was impersonating a trapeze artiste. Wobbling along with arms outstretched and singing at the top of his voice, it was obvious that he was as drunk as a lord. When I came within 50 yards of him, it all became too much for him and, after lifting his trilby in acknowledgement of the crowd, he lay down in the road and settled down to sleep.

As I was in full public view, it was clear that it was my duty to arrest him and charge him with being drunk and incapable. This presented a dilemma because if I did arrest him, instead of sampling the delights of Blackpool, the next day would be spent in the Magistrates Court. So, carrying him to the footpath, I tried to rouse him, but to no avail. I then went through his pockets because if I could find his name and address, I could get him over my shoulder and hump him home like a sack of coal. A quick check, no address. A few questions of the passersby also failed to reveal his identity. So I lifted him onto my shoulder and set off towards the police station but, after a few yards, I changed direction and turned into Ardwick Green Park, where I laid him to rest on one of the benches.

At teatime, when I strolled through the park he was still there, sound asleep and in the same position as three hours earlier. There were plenty of people about, so I chose to completely ignore him. At 8pm that evening he had gone and I breathed a sigh of relief. The Blackpool day out was saved and lived up to expectations.

More often than not, the decision not to prosecute possible offenders was exercised in favour of members of the public, with nothing else influencing the officer's judgment than the circumstances of the case and the people involved.

The police were not under such close scrutiny in those days and could operate according to their own rules. One such incident centred around a suspicious death which occurred on the C Division. The secrecy surrounding the details of the man's death was such that only a few people were privy to the actual facts and I was far too young to be counted amongst them. I am therefore relying on hearsay when I recall that close to Grey Street, Longsight, a male cyclist had indecently exposed himself and made improper suggestions to three or four small children who were playing in the street. His actions were witnessed by a group of housewives who gave chase and caught up with him, as he tried to cycle away.

During the melee, in which he was surrounded and blows were struck, the man either fell or was pushed off his cycle. As a result of the fall, he received injuries which proved fatal. Working amidst an alarmed neighbourhood, with the participants hiding behind closed doors and the non-combatants grouped on every street corner, a Sergeant calmly submitted a vehicular accident report, with no suspicious circumstances attached. The consternation and fright caused to many of those involved was so great, that the matter was still being deliberated years later ...

... Between midnight and 6am, proper duty consisted mainly of shaking hands with shop door handles and making fixed points on the beat. To relieve the boredom, many officers resorted to one of two favourite pastimes – peepshowing or boozing – both considered highly irregular, but popular nevertheless. Few of the men I knew would turn down the opportunity to take the odd glass or two whilst on duty, or to watch the occasional peepshow.

Regrettably, with about 5% of the workforce, these pursuits became obsessional. The heavy drinker would be seen making his way towards a pub or a brewery at any hour of the night or day, while the sight of a hundred watt bulb glowing in the distance would attract the dedicated peeper to it, like a moth.

I had just paraded for duty when one of the latter addicts, knowing that I was on 4 Beat, called me over before I left the station. He wanted to pass on to me information regarding his latest find. To make it appear more important, he confined himself to whispering behind a raised hand.

"Opposite Fairfield Railway Station, three terraced houses, middle one, about quarter to one – a strip off." He glanced furtively around to make sure no other officer could hear. "Climb on top of the outside toilet roof and you can see straight into the kitchen. She has a wash at the sink, biggest and best you've ever seen."

He was almost drooling at the thought of letting me in on this treat.

Those were the days before topless bathing and nudity on the television and the Manchester lads of my generation were queueing for half a mile to see the Folies Bergere at the Palace and most of them weren't there to see the dancing.

At one o'clock that morning, it was as dead as a doornail. I was due for my refreshments at 2am and, as I had an hour to kill, I thought I would give it a go. The house was easy to find and the lights were burning in both ground floor rooms. The outside toilet was in a block of three, positioned at the rear of the yard to serve the terrace of houses. I made sure that they were unoccupied by pushing the doors open and then shinning up to the roof. I wrapped my cape firmly around me and tucked my helmet under it. Even if disturbed, I would be unrecognisable as a policeman. I sat on top of the toilet roof and looked across the yard and over the half curtains into the house. A solitary figure, a buxom blonde, was playing darts. She was fully clothed, nearer to 50 than 20 and was certainly of no interest to me.

I sat cross-legged on the low roof, feeling thoroughly let down and was just about to move off, when the back door opened and the blonde came striding out. She crossed the flagged yard without seeing me and entered the toilet directly beneath me.

I cowered on top of the roof, my heart pounding after so narrow an escape, below me there was considerable groaning and straining and I now know why those outside toilets were called thunderboxes. After giving the lavatory a double flush, she finally left and re-entered the house. Whether she was going to undress, or had breasts like Marilyn Monroe, I neither knew nor cared. I clambered down from my perch and hurried away. As far as peepshowing was concerned, I was nearly cured.

The issue of whether the British Police should carry arms has long been an emotive and controversial subject. In my years of Police Service I am grateful that I was never asked to do so. Of course there is a need to train officers and to issue weapons in order to combat terrorism and other forms of armed violence. Having accompanied armed officers during the latter part of my service, I was always impressed by their composure and proficiency. As a somewhat ageing and unarmed policeman, I was chaperoned away from any probable line of fire and shielded, as far as possible, from any danger. If I have one small complaint to make, it is that I found myself being over-protected and almost molly-coddled. How times have changed!

A few nights after the episode on the toilet roof, at about one o'clock in the morning, I was standing under the pale light of a street lamp in Union Street, Ardwick, again with little to do and all night to do it in. All at once, I noticed the blazing headlights of a low dark car, swiftly sweeping along the darkened streets towards me. On seeing me, the driver jumped on the brakes and, with a loud screech, overshot me by about 20 yards and skidded to a halt on the greasy cobbles. Quickly reversing, he stopped close to me and swung open the front passenger door, in order for me to identify the occupants. I could see that it was an unmarked police car carrying the Night Crime Patrol (NCP). Every night of the week a Detective Sergeant and a Detective Constable were driven around the city by a uniformed driver, the purpose being to assist members of the uniformed branch, in all matters relating to crime.

At the driver's invitation, I leant inside the car. It smelt like a brewery. I didn't recognise any of the three men and they didn't know me. The two detectives were from other divisions and the driver was from the mobile patrol.

"Are you on this beat, Officer?" asked the one whom I later identified as the Detective Sergeant.

"Yes."

"Have you got your staff handy?" he asked unnecessarily and I nodded in confirmation.

"Jump in," he ordered, "we've got a difficult job to do and you may be needed." I sat beside the driver and half turned to face the Sergeant. "I'll tell you what's required," he continued. "We're going to arrest an American deserter. He's reported to be a bad swine and we've got information that he's armed and is now shacking up with a woman at number fifteen ... "

He named a street less than a few hundred yards away. As I sat there in the car, possibly about to embark on a dangerous mission, I felt elated – a chance to escape the boredom of the beat.

We parked the car a short distance away from where the armed deserter was allegedly holed up and covered the rest of the way on foot. As we approached the house, we became more cautious, keeping in the shadows and hugging the walls of the adjoining houses.

"This is it," whispered the Sergeant. He reeked of beer and I was certain that he was drunk. In the gloom he peered closely at my collar number. "OK, Ninety-six, get into the backyard without being heard, stand close to the back door and if he comes running out, staff the bastard."

The two detectives and the mobile patrolman stood in a cluster near the front door. The driver, being the most sober of the three, appeared to be very nervous and was surreptitiously edging himself behind the detectives.

I walked a few paces down the street, found a passageway that led to the rear of the houses and tiptoed down it. My only training for this operation came from having watched a few wartime commando films! I calculated which house was number 15 and found that the backyard gate was bolted. I entered the yard of number 11 and then, by climbing as quietly as I could over two adjoining walls, found myself in the yard at the rear of number 15. No lights were showing in the house, so I crept to the rear window and listened carefully but I couldn't hear a sound. I drew my staff and positioned myself close to the rear door, with my torch held ready in my left hand.

Then came a violent knocking on the front door, accompanied by loud shouts:

"Come down!"

"Hurry up!"

"Police!"

"Quick about it!"

I began to feel tense; if the armed deserter was going to make a run for it, he wouldn't choose the front door. The commotion soon woke the occupants of the neighbouring houses and then the upstairs lights of number 15 were switched on. I grasped my staff tighter and stood there with bated breath – it would be either now, or never. Minutes later and lights appeared in the downstairs rooms, accompanied by the sound of voices coming from the direction of the front door. Seconds passed and then someone was drawing the bolts back on the rear door. It was the mobile patrolman.

"He's not in," he blurted out breathlessly, not even pretending to be sorry. He was shaking like a leaf.

In the living-room a young woman was hastily tucking her blouse into her skirt, as she was being interviewed by the Detective Sergeant. She told him that the American had left two days earlier. The Sergeant knew this to be untrue and made her lead us round the house as we searched it, until we came the cellar. The Sergeant looked at me: "Got a torch?"

I nodded and knew what was coming next.

"Search the cellar, Ninety-six."

Fortunately there was no one there.

"All clear," I announced, as I made my way back up the cellar steps, breathing a sigh of relief.

Years later I realised how exposed I had been and how the system has changed for the benefit of all.

The policeman - Salford.   Relig.

A Strong Stomach – 15 Beat

It was Saturday morning and I was in the small kitchen at Levenshulme Section House, preparing a pair of large smoked kippers for my breakfast; a gift from my elder brother, who was on vacation in the Isle of Man. They had arrived by post the previous afternoon. The Isle of Man was a favourite holiday resort of ours and if my annual leave allocation had allowed it, I would have been there with him. He couldn't have sent a more suitable present, as kippers were one of the easiest meals to prepare in a section house.

Carrying my tea and kippers into the dining-room, I found Paddy, the jovial Station Officer, awaiting my arrival. I sat down opposite him, close to my stack of bread and butter and he stared hopefully at the food.

"Lovely kippers, Officer!"

He had a voracious appetite and was always ready to assist, should you happen to lose yours.

"Arrived from the Isle of Man yesterday afternoon. My brother's on holiday there."

"Manx kippers, eh! I should have known. They're a pair of beauties."

I took the compliment as a request and opened the pack of buttered bread.

"Fancy a kipper buttie, Paddy?"

I boned half a kipper, whilst he helped himself to two rounds of the bread and butter.

"Manx kipper. Not had one for ages," he murmured approvingly.

"It's very quiet," I said – part question, part statement, referring to the fact that no one else had joined us.

"Aye, the Sergeant's got a death. Matt's with him," he replied, as he held out the bread to be loaded with kipper.

I looked at him inquiringly.

"Not on Fifteen Beat, is it?"

"No, nothing to worry about, it's not on your beat, it's on Fourteen Beat," he assured me.

With a mouth full of kipper sandwich and in a jovial and relaxed mood, Paddy, like many Irishmen, had a fund of stories and would always start them with, "Did I ever tell you about?" This was the only line that he was guaranteed not to foul-up. For someone who knew and retold hundreds of tales, he was a dreadful story-teller. If it was a funny story, even though he may have told it dozens of times before, he would break into almost uncontrollable giggling, almost before he began, and he would splutter out the punch line in a fit of wild cackling, whilst pounding the table with his fist. When relating a serious story, it would become so convoluted that he frequently lost his way and had to reinvent the ending. Many of his anecdotes about his early days in the Force didn't stand up to close scrutiny.

On this occasion, he was telling me about his days as a young policeman when he worked under what was known as the Box System. This was a relatively inexpensive way of providing police cover in Manchester but, like many other penny-pinching systems, worked better in theory than in practice and was detested by all those who had to operate it.

When Paddy had joined the C Division in the mid-1920s, there was only the Divisional Headquarters at Mill Street and no section houses for the welfare of the men. Instead, each beat was provided with a box, big enough for two people, which was connected to the Divisional HQ by telephone. Access to the telephone could be gained either from inside or outside the box, via a small cubicle with an inner and outer door. Thus the public had immediate communication with the police and this was, perhaps, the only point in favour of the system.

The constable on the beat would parade for duty at the box and receive his working instructions via the telephone operator at Divisional HQ. After working the beat for four hours, he was then expected to take his refreshments in the box, after first scrounging a jug of boiling water, from goodness knows where, so that he could make himself a drink. After completing his eight hour stint, he then retired from duty by contacting the telephone operator. The system was extremely unpopular, as it left the policeman isolated, with no opportunity to cook food and, apart from the usually unwelcome nightly visits by the Inspector and Sergeant, without companionship. After operating for a little more than a decade, the Box System was abolished in the 1930s, having been found to be workable but unacceptable. For my generation of policemen, however, it left a most welcome bonus. On the C Division there were 30 boxes, all conveniently positioned. They gave immediate contact with Divisional HQ, shelter in a storm, a place to smoke a cigarette and a secure place in which to detain a prisoner, whilst summoning the Black Maria.

Paddy launched into his story.

"Did I ever tell you about when I was working under the Box System?"

The story concerned a cheeky, foul-mouthed, young lad, who regularly played truant from school and was normally seen wandering the streets of Ancoats, with a catapult hanging out of his jacket pocket. After a couple of hours' light target practice at the neighbourhood cats, he would stick his catapult back into his pocket and wander off to Butler Street, where he would give a load of old buck to the shopkeepers who knew him well.

On this particular morning, he was having a lot to say to an elderly greengrocer, who had interrupted him as he was about to steal an apple. Whilst he was busy slagging off the greengrocer and telling him, not only where to shove his apples, but his water melons as well, Paddy had come up behind him and caught him by the ear. To teach him a lesson, and to make him aware of the seriousness of his behaviour, he led him away, still by the ear, to the nearest police box and locked him up. Knowing the strength of Paddy's banana-like fingers, I should imagine that this would have been an extremely painful process.

After leaving the boy in the box for an hour or so, to give him time to reflect and, maybe, repent of his misdeeds, Paddy returned to release him.

"Have you learnt your lesson?"

"Yes, Sir."

"You're sure?"

"Yes, Sir, definitely."

"You wont do it again?"

"No, Sir, honest."

"Are you going back to school on your own, or shall I take you?"

"I'll go on my own, Sir. Trust me."

"Well, off you go and don't let me catch you giving cheek again. Not to anyone mind."

When the lad was about ten yards away from the box, he turned and shouted at Paddy:

"Piss off you big fat Irish sod and take a look at your drawer. I've eaten all your soddin' butties."

A good story, but yet another one which didn't stand up to close scrutiny. All the box doors were equipped with the standard Yale lock. At any time the boy could have simply let himself out by opening the door from the inside – a key was only needed to open the door from the outside!

Paddy had just finished his tale, when in walked the Sergeant, looking quite pale and out of sorts. He nodded at us and removed his helmet, before examining the contents of my tea jug. Satisfied with what he saw, he took a cup out of the cupboard and helped himself to my tea, without asking if it was alright. Knowing that he should be still engaged elsewhere with the sudden death report, Paddy asked,

"Everything OK, Sarge?"

The Sergeant gulped at the tea, as if washing a nasty taste out of his mouth.

"Anything but," he answered, "it's a really awful mess," and he looked across at me, as if I was his last hope. "I need your help, Ninety-six. Have you got a strong stomach?"

"Fairly," I replied cautiously, not sure whether I had or not.

The Sergeant was a clever, conscientious type, whose feet were now on the first rung of the promotion ladder. Later he was to advance high in the Service though, sadly, he died whilst still a comparatively young man.

Anyway, he finished the tea and placed the empty cup on the table with an emphatic gesture.

"When you're ready then. I'll tell you about it on the way down."

He looked at me steadily, trying to decide whether I was up to the task. I buttoned up by tunic and reached for my helmet.

"Ready when you are, Sarge."

We left the station, crossed the main Stockport Road and were walking quickly along the footpath towards 14 Beat before he spoke and then it was in short broken sentences, his mind on the job ahead.

"Ruddy awful situation … old woman lived alone … died in the bath … not been seen for three months … no relatives … neighbours alarmed at the number of bluebottles in the area."

I kept pace with him and chanced a sideways glance – he still looked deathly pale. He caught me looking at him.

"I broke into her house about an hour ago," he grimaced. "Could hardly move for the bluebottles. I opened all the windows and for minutes afterwards they were like a black cloud, buzzing round the garden."

He increased his pace and turned to look straight ahead, his stick tapping the pavement.

"She's naked in the bath tub … no water in it … must weigh eighteen stone … badly decomposed … flesh stuck to the bath enamel … can't budge her at all." He named the constable who was supposed to be helping him. "Matt's not the man for the job – he did his best … had to run outside … sick as a dog … can't expect any more from him."

A vivid picture of what lay in store was forming in my mind.

"Oh, I forgot to mention … bath's absolutely teeming with maggots."

Curiously enough, distasteful as it may be, I was looking forward to a job which would test my mettle and allow me to prove myself. Before joining the Force I had spent three years helping to design coal-washing plants and from this experience I was about to make my first useful contribution.

"Soon shift the maggots with a hosepipe. Flush 'em down the drain. Then we can fill the bath – see if we can get some buoyancy."

At this, the Sergeant turned to look at me with the first real gleam of hope in his eyes and we proceeded to the house in silence. It was a small, pre-war semi and grouped close to the front gate, were a dozen or so of the deceased's neighbours, talking amongst themselves. Standing in the roadway outside, was the black mortuary van, with a solitary attendant at the wheel. He was staring ahead in a manner which made it plain that he certainly wasn't going to help.

We entered the house and out of the dining-room window saw Matt, the 14 beat man, in the back garden. From the way he was examining the flowers, I could tell that he wasn't going to be of any assistance to us.

In situations such as this, it is the duty of the police to have the death certified and then arrange for the body to be removed to the mortuary. The doctor had certified the death with one glance. Now for the removal and that was to be our job.

The sight in the bathroom was ghastly and the smell utterly appalling. We only had one pair of rubber gloves between us. I used my uniform white cotton gloves and later threw them away. The next hour was a struggle in that small enclosed room. A nauseating experience I would not wish to repeat. But the job had to be done. Obviously, there was no official word of praise for either of us. But the Sergeant's words were enough for me:

"You'll do me, son."

Nothing more, but as far as one person was concerned, I had made my mark.

At one end of 15 Beat, the main A6 road leaves the city and enters the borough of Stockport and unless you noticed the signs placed at the boundary, you wouldn't know that you had passed from one district into another. Green and open land had previously separated the two townships but had been gobbled up before urban planning and the Green Belt were ever dreamed about. Close to this point, within the city boundary, is a small triangle of grassland on which stood a small bus depot, a garage and a blue police box.

It was a Saturday afternoon in September and summer was still clinging on and we were enjoying an unbroken spell of sunshine and clear blue skies. If I had been a country bobby, it would have been all too tempting to lean on an old gate and watch the world go by. But working in a city had its compensations, particularly in relation to policework.

Standing close to the police box, with my back to the triangle of grassland, I ran my fingers under the collar of my tunic and, with my handkerchief, wiped the perspiration from inside the band of my helmet. No thought had been given to issuing light-weight uniforms and on those hot summer days we had to sweat it out in navy-blue serge. A bus heading out of the city drew up at the nearby stop and an elderly lady started to alight.

"Cringle Road, ma," called out the conductor, pointing out the road which ran at a tangent to the main A6. That it required a bus conductor to direct an elderly lady to her destination seemed slightly unusual and caused me to look at her more closely, as she made her way slowly along Cringle Road.

I estimated that she was closer to 90 than 80, that she had once been tall and slim but now looked stooped and frail. She had a serious yet gentle face and wisps of white hair strayed from under her knitted hat. Despite the weather, she was wearing a heavy blue topcoat, which almost reached to her ankles. Hooked over the crook of her left arm was an old-fashioned wicker shopping basket, whilst clutched tightly in her right hand, was a worn leather purse. After walking for a few yards, she paused to peep into the shopping basket and I noticed it was covered with a white napkin. After another few steps, she stopped and looked about her, a bewildered expression on her face. She was obviously lost and I had already decided to speak to her when she suddenly turned round and came slowly towards me, looking very anxious. I walked towards her and when we met, I caught her gently by the arm, to prevent her from attempting to cross the busy road.

"Is everything alright, dear?" She nodded but looked away from me, as if searching for someone or something. "Do you want to cross the road?" I asked her softly.

"I don't know," she answered, in a shaky voice. "I'm looking for Cringle Fields, but I can't find them."

At the top of Cringle Road, behind a small estate of pre-war houses, was a small open space which was known locally as Cringle Fields, but I had the feeling that this was not what she had in mind.

"Do you live nearby?" I asked.

She extended the arm which held the wicker basket.

"Oh, no. I've come for a picnic."

"I wonder if I could have a look in your basket," I asked her, and when she proffered it to me, I peeped under the napkin. It was just as I thought: a cup, saucer, plate and cutlery for a single-place setting. She smiled at me faintly.

"I've come to the Fields for a picnic. It's a lovely day, isn't it?"

I agreed.

"Could I now have a look inside your purse?" I asked her.

She handed me the purse and inside I found a piece of white card on which was printed: 'My name is Mrs Smiley. If found wandering, please contact this address.'

The name and address was that of Mrs Smiley's daughter, who lived in Urmston, many miles away, on the other side of the city. There was no telephone number, which wasn't surprising, because, in those days, only a few people were connected to the system. Now it would be necessary to get in touch with Mrs Smiley's daughter through the police office at Urmston.

"Shall we go for a bus ride?"

She nodded enthusiastically, as though this had happened before. We soon boarded a bus which took us to Levenshulme Section House. I had already contacted Paddy to let him know we were coming and, as the bus pulled up, he was standing on the footpath outside. He greeted her like a long-lost relative.

"Why, Mrs Smiley, come on in and sit yourself down, dearie. It's quite a time since I've seen you. Are you keeping well?"

She smiled at him, obviously pleased at the warmth of her reception.

"Yes, I'm keeping quite well. Thank you."

Paddy took her arm and escorted her inside.

"Lovely weather we've been having, Mrs Smiley. I see you've got your basket with you. Have you come for a picnic?"

"Yes, but I can't find the Fields, and yet they should be there. I asked the bus conductor to put me off at Cringle Road, like we always did."

Having seated her at the dining-room table, we went into the small office to make the necessary arrangements for her to be collected.

"She's ninety-three," said Paddy. "A grand old girl for her age but her memory's going. The family were business people in the city, something to do with cotton and she used to come to Levenshulme eighty years ago, when it was considered to be in the country. All her family would come down to Cringle Fields and spend the day picnicking by the brook. How times have changed!"

I handed him the purse and he took out the white address card.

"Still living in Urmston I see." He was soon on the telephone to the police office there. "Yes, that's right, Officer, Levenshulme Section House. Don't worry, Mrs Smiley's daughter knows where it is well enough, she's a regular customer."

In the dining-room, Mrs Smiley had laid out her picnic on the table and was now straightening the creases out of the white napkin. Paddy smiled, then put on his helmet.

"Just watch the station for a minute or two, Ninety-six, and make a cup of tea whilst I'm gone."

By the time the tea was brewed, he was back with a bag full of cakes. He set out six small fancies on the table in front of Mrs Smiley.

"We'll let you be mother," he smiled, nodding towards the teapot.

Mrs Smiley poured the tea and proffered the cakes in a motherly fashion. She was going to have her picnic after all.

Little Porkers wi' Sticky Up Ears – 16 Beat

Dog licences were first introduced by the Government as a form of taxation, to raise revenues to fight the Napoleonic wars but were not abolished until 1986. During the 170 odd years between, the licence fee remained the same, at seven shillings and sixpence, or thirty seven and a half pence in decimal currency. There were, of course, exemptions, such as guide dogs for the blind, sheep dogs, hounds under 12 months old when used in a pack and puppies under the age of six months. So, broadly speaking, unless otherwise exempt, when a dog reached the age of six months, the owner was expected to go along to the post office and take out a licence.

Remarkable for a division where there were no sheep dogs or hounds and precious few guide dogs in its vast canine population, there were very few licences taken out in the C. There was a ratio of ten dogs per licence issued. This always presented a problem for officers who didn't want to go to court with trivial offences, in this case nicknamed, Rex versus Rex.

Problems usually arose when the unlicensed animal had either been killed or injured in a road accident. To comply with the Road Traffic Act, an accident report had to be submitted and in order for him to complete the report, the Police Officer had to furnish the particulars of the dog licence. Then, at the home of the injured dog, often with the injured animal whining at the officer as it lay on the pegged rug in front of the coal fire or, when the dog had been killed, in front of a cluster of tearful children, there would follow a fruitless search through the sideboard drawers by the worried owner, a hopeful root in the toby jug, a sideways glance at an anxious wife and, ultimately, a sad shake of the head.

The officer would, under normal circumstances, make the necessary adjustment to the animal's age, in order to bring it under the required six months, sometimes reducing its lifespan by as much as 12 years. A Manchester Chief Constable once reported that five months was a dangerous age for dogs living in the city.

Whenever I think of 16 Beat, I think of dogs. Not that there were more dogs on 16 Beat, it was just the way things seemed to work out. The beat was in Levenshulme and, like 15 Beat, extended to the Stockport boundary, with the A6 separating them. I enjoyed working in Levenshulme; for me it meant spending an hour less in travel each day and consequently an hour less on duty. Travelling to work, either by bike or public transport, was always in full uniform. Once in uniform, I was on duty and this meant that a careful authority got more out of me than they paid for: two hours a day when travelling to stations other than Levenshulme. It was always annoying, when travelling home from work at 10.30 at night, to become involved in a 'drunk and disorderly', or a serious accident.

Levenshulme was considered to be the up-market part of the division. Although it was a busy, built-up area, it was less industrialised than other areas in the C and was known to policemen as Sleepy Valley; something which the older bobbies never let Paddy forget, particularly when he was telling them how busy he had been.

One hot sunny morning, with the summer still clinging on, I was relaxing in the Section House, after finishing my refreshments. Paddy sat opposite and, as usual, had helped himself to a cup of tea and a bacon sandwich. He was in a jovial mood and was relating tales about 'auld Oirland' and the small village near Donegal where he had been born. His tales were always worth repeating and this one concerned their local Garda Sergeant and his constable who, shortly after the turn of the century, arrested a 'diddy-can' (a tinker or a vagrant) for being drunk and incapable. As a stranger to the neighbourhood, they placed him somewhat unceremoniously in a small cell where, during the night, he died. For the Sergeant, this was particularly worrying because neither man was skilled with the pen and an exacting coroner's report had to be written. He made several attempts at it but never got past the first line: Sergeant Thomas Sean O'Casey begs to report.

Just before dawn, the good Sergeant O'Casey and his constable picked up the dead vagrant, took him to the bottom of the long garden and buried him. I smiled when Paddy finished telling the story, his eyes were twinkling and he was looking at me, as if he had been caught telling tales out of school.

He was in the midst of yet another story about a young Irish policeman who, after cooking his refreshments, tried to blow the gas out, when someone walked through the permanently open door of the Section House into the front office, bringing with him an appalling smell. Paddy smiled and held his nose between finger and thumb in a jocular fashion. He rose from his chair, wrinkled his nose and pretended to stagger from the effects of the smell, as he walked out of the dining-room to see who had arrived.

After a few moments, during which time I could hear him conversing with someone, he poked his head round the corner of the door and called me into the office. Standing next to him was a stout, middle-aged man and it was he who had brought the raw smell of the countryside into the section house. He wore a flat cap with the peak bent upwards and under a ruddy, weather-beaten face, and firmly knotted round his throat, was a silk scarf, once white but now muck-stained and turning a brownish-green colour. Twenty years earlier his buttonless raincoat had possibly been fashioned out of gabardine. It was neither fawn, blue, grey or black, but it definitely matched the colour of his scarf. A length of binding cord, which had been tied around his waist, prevented the coat from flapping open. Most of the foul smell seemed to come from his wellington boots, which were encrusted with layers of pig muck. I smiled at the man and his face broke into a broad grin.

"Ow do, squire,"

It was Piggy Pilling, once seen, rarely forgotten, and Paddy started to formally introduce us.

"Now, Officer, this is Mr Pilling. He has a smallholding at the end of your beat. Mr Pilling, this is C Ninety-six. He's the Officer in charge of your beat."

Formality was not Paddy's strong point and he was obviously very self-conscious of the pig manure collecting on his polished floor.

"Now, Piggy, tell the young man what the problem is - if he can help you, he will."

I suspect that, deep down, Piggy Pilling was a bogus countryman, for when he spoke, his accent was a mixture of several Shire counties, with a dash of Long John Silver, similar to the men who call on town and city dwellers in the spring and autumn to sell them horse manure and leave them with bags of urine-soaked straw.

What Mr Pilling had to tell me concerned canine lust at its worst.

"Sloike this, squire, 'barrassing really," he began in his booming voice. "Bluddy big Alsatian's comin' an' rapin' me sows. Sodden girt swoine he be, ins 'em and outs 'em and then pisses off, afore I can get to 'im. I'd shoot the girt bastard but oi's 'ave no gun an' oi's not the killin' toipe."

I found it difficult to keep a straight face.

"And when does this happen, Mr Pilling?"

Now he reverted to his Long John Silver bit. He had obviously seen Robert Newton in the part, for he tried to roll his eyes but ended up merely lifting his eyelids and looking sideways.

"Ye name it, squire, and 'e be there. Jumps o'er bluddy fence loike a Gran' National winner. Ah doubts if there's one o' buggers 'e's not 'ad it off wi'."

Paddy suddenly found his tongue.

"Nasty business, Piggy, nasty business. We'll have to put a stop to it."

As Paddy rarely left the station, it was obvious that it would be my responsibility to bring law and order to the sty.

"I'll certainly give it special attention, Mr Pilling."

This assurance implied much but in reality meant very little.

"An grateful oi be, squire," he bellowed, "could be bad for business tha knows."

"How's that, Mr Pilling?"

"Well just think on it, squire. All that seed bugger's plantin'. There's no market for little porkers wi' sticky up ears tha knows." With that he bade us farewell, in true country fashion, by touching his forelock. "Oi be off now, squire," he said to Paddy. "See you later, young sir," he called to me and set off to retrieve the ladies cycle, which he had propped against the wall.

Like his wellington boots, the cycle was also encrusted in rich pig manure, with hardly a spoke visible. He rode away with his coat flapping about his wellingtons, heading down the A6 in the direction of his piggery; a most unusual sight.

I called in at the piggery a couple of hours later. It was easy to find because you quite literally followed your nose. In the countryside, such smells would have virtually gone unnoticed but here in the city they were quite distinctive and, as I approached the gates, the effluvium almost dragged me inside. Piggy was seated on an orange box, mixing swill. Whether the pigs had been affected by the 'rapin', it was difficult to say. To my inexperienced eyes they looked perfectly happy and when Piggy sloshed the swill into their trough, I noticed that they hadn't been put off their food.

"Has he been back, Mr Pilling?" I asked.

"Not as oi knows abaht but th'owd sod's such a crafty un, he's up and away afore I knows he's abaht place," he replied, dropping his swill bucket with a clang.

The following day I gave the smallholding my special attention - walking round it slowly and letting the uniform be seen. Not that I expected a lovesick Alsatian to take much notice.

On the third day, as I approached the piggery, I spotted the culprit heading towards me, practically on tiptoe. He was far bigger than the average Alsatian - more the size of a timber-wolf. His tail tucked firmly between his legs, his jaws gaping wide and tongue lolling out of one side of his mouth, he had a look of utter exhaustion in his eyes, mingled with undisguised lust. He was plastered from head to tail in pig manure. He overtook me without a glance, totally unaware of my special interest in his case and the smell, as he passed, was worse than Piggy Pilling's wellington boots. There wasn't a jury in the land who wouldn't have convicted him on sight! He headed towards the piggery, full of carnal intent. He wasn't a pretty sight and I began to realise my limitations. Attempting to part this amorous Alsatian from a fully-grown sow, in the middle of a filthy pigsty, whilst dressed in best day uniform, would mean there would be no winners, only losers, and I didn't intend to be one of them.

Policemen excel in awarding nicknames to less fortunate colleagues, some of them very cruel indeed and such an incident could generate untold possibilities in a fertile mind - it didn't bear thinking about. If the dog had fallen in love with the pigs, that was his business. As far as I was concerned, regulating the flow of traffic on the busy A6 was my business and I made my way there, confident in the knowledge that I wasn't increasing the risk of Mr Pilling raising a litter of 'little porkers wi' sticky up ears'.

□ □ □ □

ROE - Right, Odd, Early and the Mode of Working was one point right. I was on nights and due in for my refreshments late. If this sounds complicated, I assure you that it isn't.

On C Division we were working the fixed point system. On each beat there were four points. Imagine a square with corners numbered one to four. The square was the beat and the numbered corners were the fixed points. The method of working varied daily. If working right, then the beat was worked in a clockwise direction, moving from one point to two point and then on to three and four. If working left, the beat was patrolled anti-clockwise, moving from one point to four point and from there to three and to two points. Working right and the inside of the beat had to be kept on your right side; working left and it was the reverse.

On nights, we were allowed 45 minutes between points and on days, 30 minutes. The number, in the Mode of Working, indicated the point at which the patrol commenced. If on nights, the mode was one point right. The beat would commence at one point at 10pm and move on to two point for 10.45pm. When the Mode of Working was right (clockwise), then the odd numbered beats took early refreshments. I was on 16 Beat and we were working one point right, so I was due in for late supper at 2am.

However, everything doesn't always work to plan and, at 2am, I was in the home of a young couple who were very distressed. They had arrived home from a dinner dance, excited and happy, only to find that their house had been broken into and some of their treasured possessions stolen. I helped them to make the house secure, comforted them as best I could by mentioning their insurance policy, and persuaded them to go to bed, as little more could be done until the following morning, when enquiries would be made to ascertain whether their neighbours had seen anyone acting suspiciously.

Women, particularly, are difficult to reassure when someone has intruded into the privacy of their home and it is not easy for them to put the experience out of their minds. To the housebreaker, this aspect of the crime means little but, to the householder, it is the worst part of the offence. It is not much use suggesting that lightning never strikes twice in the same place, for it does. Certain houses are particularly prone to house-breaking and it can become a regular event, often causing great distress. Perhaps the sooner that certain judges and magistrates take into account such feelings and stop pussyfooting when it comes to the punishment of offenders, the better society will be for it.

At 4am I had finished my sandwiches and was still at the dining-room table, completing the crime report. Paddy had finished his housework and was sitting opposite me. The table had been cleared, the crockery washed and stacked in the cupboard, the pans had been scrubbed and, finally, the floors had been polished. The three Section House Officers were responsible for cleaning the building and, under the threat of being sent out to work on the beat again, took the job very seriously. They worked well together. Each morning the floors would be swept, each afternoon they would be washed and each night they would be polished, by which time, they were as slippery as an ice-rink.

I was hunched over my report, chatting to Paddy. He had obviously heard it all before because, when I next looked up, he had fallen fast asleep and this on an uncomfortable, hardbacked chair. He was sprawled precariously, with his back and shoulders resting on the wall behind him. The two front legs of the chair were clear of the floor, at an angle of 45 degrees. His hands were interlocked and resting on his generous stomach, the top two buttons of his trouser-fly were undone, forming a V and he was breathing gently. Every now and again he gave the hint of a snore. His face was broad, pleasant and homely - a real guileless Irish face. He was a man without malice, the ideal choice of Station Officer for Sleepy Valley.

On this warm night, every door in the station was wide open, as were the outer doors of the dog kennels. Only the big iron gate was locked. Little consideration was given to security in my early days on the Force. We were there to protect the public and to provide a service. Any thoughts that we could possibly be the victims of terrorists never occurred to us, nor would it do so for several years to come.

Suddenly, in the stillness of the night, I heard the patter of tiny feet. I glanced up from my report and looked towards the sound. A small brown and white puppy had entered the dining-room and was standing just inside the door, its head cocked to one side. It seemed to be seeking human company.

"Hello," I said, in a hushed voice, "have you come to see us?"

The puppy wagged its tail, but didn't move. Paddy opened one eye to see who I was talking to and saw the puppy. He then opened the other eye and rubbed the sleep away with his sausage-like fingers, while waiting for his brain to kick into gear. When it did, he sprang into action, letting out a roar and, at the same time, trying to right himself on his chair.

"Grab the dog!" he shouted, struggling to bring the four legs of his chair back onto terra firma.

The commotion caused the puppy to panic. It turned and started to run as fast as it could, but without achieving any forward motion. The floor was so highly polished that it couldn't find the necessary purchase to get started and its rear legs were spinning round like a couple of Catherine-wheels.

"He's got out of the kennels," bellowed Paddy. "Catch him, quick!"

He managed to right his chair but was struggling to regain his feet. Just then, the puppy managed to dig his claws into the linoleum and was off like a rocket out of the section house. We both rushed to the front door but it was too late. He had turned left along the footpath and left again as he raced across the car-park of the local Palais and out of sight.

We checked the kennels, hoping that Paddy had been mistaken, but they were empty. Worse still was the fact that there had been an element of neglect on Paddy's part. Although the puppy had squeezed through the bars of the kennel, the outer door had been left wide open.

"Jesus," he murmured, "we'll have to find him."

It was panic stations as he imagined his plum job in jeopardy. It wasn't the puppy's escape that was causing him to panic, it was the paperwork and the inability to balance the books. There was an entry in the dog register made out in Paddy's best handwriting, 'Found - one brown and white male puppy dog'. No puppy, therefore no receipt from the man who called daily from the dog's home to collect any strays. When the superintendent inspected the journals on his weekly visit, the following Sunday morning, no discrepancy would escape his eagle eye. Paddy would be for the high jump! Paddy knew all this and it spurred him into action.

"Come on," he ordered. "Get your helmet on. There's nothing else for it, we'll have to find him."

We searched high and low, without success. There was no trace of the little blighter anywhere. By a quarter to five, Paddy was really agitated - soon it would be daylight.

"Any brown and white one will do," he snapped.

But we couldn't find a dog of any description. Normally there would be quite a number of strays about and children always seemed to be bringing them to the station.

By 5.15am I knew that Paddy was becoming desperate, when he called me by my first name.

"Any dog will do, Tony, don't worry about the size or colour. I'll square it with the dog man."

By 5.30 a light drizzle had begun to fall and we had donned our capes and were now searching in streets a quarter of a mile away from the section house. Soon the morning relief would be arriving and we only had half an hour to find a dog and so save Paddy's bacon. Then his prayers were answered and providence came to our aid. The door of a small terraced house opened a few inches and a pair of hands appeared, pushing a small dog out into the drizzle for its morning walk. Paddy pounced on the tiny thing and bundled it under his cape.

"Get the house number," he whispered, conspiratorially, whilst trying to comfort the struggling animal. We quickly made our way back to the station to examine our find. It was a black and tan bitch. Not ideal, but the best we could do.

"Don't worry about its colour or sex," said Paddy, impatiently, "I'll square that up later."

He put the bitch in the kennels and, to make doubly sure that there would be no further escape, he closed and bolted the outer door. He wrote the dog's address on a piece of paper and handed it to the friendly officer who relieved him, explaining the position and ended by saying:

"Tell them that we've got their dog in our kennels and get them to collect it."

Parading for duty at ten o'clock that night, I peeped into the kennels, expecting that the black and tan bitch would be long gone. No, she was still there and jumped to her feet when she saw me, wagging her tail, as if anticipating a treat. I then noticed that she was surrounded by titbits.

Apparently, during the day, when the story had leaked out amongst the various policemen, they had made her their pet and she now expected to be fussed over by all and sundry. A few minutes later I was discussing the situation with Paddy, making arrangements to get the dog back home and even offering to take her there myself, if necessary. Whilst we were conferring, a man walked into the station, whistling cheerfully.

"Good evening, Officer," he called to Paddy, "I believe you've got our dog here. I've just been out for a pint and thought I'd pick her up on the way home."

"Come this way, Sir," said Paddy and led the owner to the kennels, where there was a joyful reunion with the little bitch leaping almost shoulder high. "Nice little dog," commented Paddy, stroking her affectionately.

"Yes, she's a friendly little thing," replied the owner, "but I'm surprised she wandered off. She's rarely more than ten yards away from the front doorstep. Beats me how you knew she was ours. Only there's no name tag on her collar - been meaning to get one for ages."

Paddy wasn't the least bit put out.

"Surprising what we do know, Sir. Not much escapes our notice when we're patrolling the streets."

The owner was suitably impressed.

"Good God! Have to watch myself then. I didn't know you were that efficient."

Paddy led the way back into the office and placed the opened dog register on top of the long desk.

"Just sign here, Sir," he said, covering the part that read, brown and white male puppy dog, with a large gnarled Irish hand.

The man took up the pen and signed trustingly. This left just one more formality, a slightly awkward one for us. Paddy coughed into his hand in embarrassment.

"There's a shilling to pay, Sir. It's for the biscuits and keep. I'm sorry about that, regulations you know."

The man paid the shilling with a smile.

"Worth every penny. I'm only too pleased she's been so well looked after."

Paddy caught my eye; his conscience was obviously troubling him. He bent down and patted the dog.

"Aye, she's a nice little thing and she certainly enjoys our biscuits." He straightened his back as he sought to salve his conscience. "Just a moment, Sir." He walked to the kennels and came back with a large bag of dog biscuits and thrust them into the man's hand. "Here, take these with you. Help to keep her going for a while."

We stepped out of the station and watched the man leading his dog home. Paddy rubbed his hands with pleasure.

"Job well done, Tony," he said, looking happy and relaxed once again in Sleepy Valley, "job well done."

We had just changed over from nights to afternoons, retiring from duty at 6am that Sunday morning and returning at 2pm. This sort of quick changeover badly affected many of us, leaving us feeling liverish and bad-tempered. Paddy was 'weekend off' and the section house was manned by a 'knob stick'; the name given to those who relieved specialist officers on a regular basis. Stan was the knob stick now in charge of the section house. He was a dark, extremely thin and sallow-complexioned individual, who suffered from stomach ulcers, high blood pressure and bronchial trouble. As a policeman, apart from being conscientious, he didn't particularly have a lot going for him, especially as he was the most bad-tempered person, even at the best of times.

Responsible for 15 Beat, which ran parallel to mine, was Gerry, who was even younger and less experienced than me. Normally a sensible and fun-loving character, he was now completely out of sorts. Apparently, shortly after arriving for duty, he had become involved in a dispute with Stan, over the ownership of a pair of uniform gloves. Neither of them was prepared to give ground and the argument became so heated that it required the Sergeant to end it skilfully, without taking sides. Gerry had the more honest claim but Stan had the right of possession and was consequently in an advantageous position. After the slanging match, Stan had thrown the gloves into a drawer, which he locked, telling Gerry to sling his hook but using only two words. A few minutes later, when Gerry and I were on our way out of the station to begin our respective beats, we passed the office door. Stan was aware of our presence but refused to look at us and instead tried to bury himself behind a copy of the News of the World.

We moved away along Stockport Road and Gerry, smarting under a sense of injustice, was still very angry.

"They're my gloves," he insisted convincingly, "I left them in the parade room when I retired this morning. That sod's only just found them. They're mine and he bloody well knows it. 'Bout time they pensioned the stupid old git off."

Half a mile later, with no sign of Gerry's temper cooling off, we approached 37 Box, which stood opposite St Peter's Church.

"I'll give him something to think about," muttered Gerry and, with that, we crossed the road and entered the box.

Gerry was an excellent mimic and had few equals in his ability to take off the nobility or members of the clergy, from the Archbishop downwards. His speciality act was his reading of the wedding service.

We settled into the box and Gerry grimly nodded at me.

"Watch this," he said.

He was showing signs of recovering his composure and allowed himself to smile at the thought of retaliation. He lifted the old-fashioned telephone out of its box and placed it on the counter in front of us. It was the heavy metal upright type, with a separate earpiece and mouthpiece. He lifted the earpiece off the stand, allowing the lever to click up, giving us immediate contact with Divisional Headquarters at Mill Street. We stood sharing the earphone, grinning at each other like a couple of schoolboys playing a prank on the master.

"Mill Street Police Station," answered the operator.

"Good afternoon," said Gerry, "would you kindly put me in touch with the police station at Levenshulme."

"Certainly, Sir."

After a short pause, we heard a click and the sound of Stan's voice: "Levenshulme."

Gerry's accent was straight out of the top drawer.

"Is that the police at Levenshulme?"

"Yes, police at Levenshulme," replied Stan.

"Oh, good. This is the vicar of St Peter's speaking."

Stan seemed suitably impressed and replied very politely.

"Oh, good afternoon, Vicar."

"Hardly a good afternoon, Officer," said Gerry, an edge creeping into the upper crust voice.

"Oh, and why ever not?"

"Why not?" retorted Gerry, crisply, "I'll tell you why not. Because something indecent's happening down here."

"Indecent?"

"Yes, grossly indecent," complained Gerry.

"What's that then, Vicar?"

"I have to report that there are two dogs fornicating."

"Fornicating?" stammered Stan in a surprised voice.

"Yes, fornicating. Between what looks like a cross-breed border collie and a white Sealyham," continued Gerry, as if he was a regular attender at Crufts.

"What are they actually doing?" asked Stan, playing for time.

"They're fornicating. You do understand what that means don't you, Officer?"

Gerry spoke rather condescendingly, knowing full well that this would needle Stan.

"Aye, I know what you mean right enough, but what do you expect me to do about it?"

"Do about it? I want you to come down here immediately and stop them. I expect you to do your duty."

Stan tried to appease him.

"Now, Vicar, they're only performing a natural function."

"A natural function! Good gracious me, man. Do you for one moment realise what you're saying?" Gerry's voice became even more scandalised. "The animals are fornicating on a Sunday afternoon, on the footpath immediately outside St Peters, in full view of all the Sunday school children and you call that a natural function."

"Yes, but they don't realise all that," said Stan, springing to the animals' defence. "To them it's a natural function."

"They're fornicating and I want something done to stop them. I've finished listening to silly excuses from a silly man."

Stan's voice sounded very agitated.

"Don't you realise that I'm a very busy person. I have other more important duties to perform."

Now he was hiding behind an imaginary workload.

"A busy man, indeed!" responded Gerry, "I shouldn't imagine that you understand the meaning of the words. You're probably sitting there reading the Sunday newspaper. By the sound of your voice, the News of the World, I shouldn't wonder."

"Now listen here, Vicar," spluttered Stan.

"I've no intention of listening to you any more my good man. I insist that you come and separate these animals immediately."

"I can't leave the station," Stan protested, "I've duties to perform. And before you say any more - I couldn't give a damn whether it's Sunday, Monday or Tuesday, whether they're dogs or elephants, or whether they're performing outside St Peters, or inside the bloody Vatican!"

"I insist that you come and separate them," replied Gerry sharply.

"Insist all you want, Vicar. If it's that important to you, why don't you just throw a bucket of water over them?"

"I'll have you know that I am preparing for my afternoon service. Would you really expect a man of God to rush out of his church in his surplice and throw a bucket of water over a pair of dogs?" Gerry raised his voice slightly. "Quite frankly, I'm disgusted with your attitude."

"Be that as it may ... "

Suddenly Gerry allowed his voice to become excited.

"I know who you are now. I recognise your voice. You're the bad-tempered gentleman with the disgraceful reputation, aren't you?"

Stan's temper blew.

"Now Vicar, I'm putting this phone down. Either throw a bucket of water on them, or else go back into the church and ignore them."

"Before you put the phone down, I'm warning you, there'll be a letter of complaint to the Chief Constable. I shall send it by the first post tomorrow."

"Complain all you want," shouted Stan.

"It will be written on church notepaper," threatened Gerry.

"Umph!"

With that, Stan slammed down the phone.

I called in at the section house shortly before teatime. Stan was sitting, hunched up, in the dining-room, staring ahead with the News of the World folded on the table in front of him. His face was purple and blotchy - he'd obviously had a difficult afternoon.

"Everything OK, Stan?"

He rose from the table and walked into the office to be on his own. "Soddin' vicars and soddin' dogs," he blurted out. "Sod the lot of 'em."

Starkers – 21 Beat

The 24 hour policing of 21 Beat consisted of two different undertakings. During the hours of daylight it was regarded as just another working-class beat in Gorton but at night the policeman's duties were confined to patrolling Cross Street and Wellington Street, two small connecting streets of lock-up shops, which were the forerunner of today's shopping precincts and considered to be vulnerable targets for criminals.

During the hours of darkness it was certainly boring, repeatedly walking up and down the lines of back entries, making sure that the rear of the properties were secure and then patrolling up and down the front, ensuring that that aspect was also in order. Studying the displays in the shop windows, by torchlight, gave a little light relief but, after a fortnight, every article was familiar.

To make it easy for the policemen checking the rear of their property, some of the shopkeepers had bored peepholes in the back gates. The ideal arrangement was two holes, each about nine inches in diameter, spaced about a foot apart and about five feet six inches from the ground. These allowed a torch to be pushed through one gap, whilst looking through the other to see if everything was in order.

Needless to say, many of the shopkeepers had peculiar ideas as to this requirement. Sometimes one hole, two inches in diameter, would be drilled into the gate, six feet six inches from the ground, by a shopkeeper who must have thought that all policemen had descended from Goliath. You had to grasp the top edge of the gate, lever yourself up to peephole level, whilst, at the same time, pushing your torch over the gate to try to give everywhere a coating of light.

Then there was the other extreme. A certain shopkeeper in Cross Street must have employed a midget to bore his single, small peephole, for it was no more than three feet from the ground, which was fine if you happened to be a contortionist. If so, you might be able to bend down and peep through the hole and, at the same time, push the torch over the top edge of the gate and illuminate the yard. Being still young and reasonably fit, I could just about manage to do this, but knew that in doing so I was leaving myself exposed to attack by the very criminals I was seeking. I was not nervous, but realistically aware of the danger which existed and this was the property I least preferred to check.

On one occasion, around midnight, I walked down the darkened back passageway to check the property and arrived at the gate in question. I bent down to inspect the premises, which entailed performing the usual contortions and, whilst in this defenceless position, I was aware of a slight movement behind me. Someone brushed past me and then a hand fell onto my shoulder. I now know how shock affects me; I go weak at the knees, momentarily stop breathing, practically lose control of my bladder, my scalp prickles and I feel as though I've been punched under the heart.

"It's alright, Sir. I've examined the backs of these shops – they're all in order," came a squeaky female voice.

I spun round and slumped against the gate. Shining my torch into the face of the speaker, I found myself looking at a middle-aged lady, just over five feet in height. She wore a belted raincoat, a headscarf and a pair of ankle-length galoshes. In one hand she carried a torch and in the other a small umbrella. It was K11. Perhaps it was a good job I had also lost my voice!

It was Kay who made doubly sure that central Gorton was one of the best policed districts in Manchester. Apparently, she was going through the menopause and one of her symptoms was insomnia. To spend her sleepless nights usefully and to make them pass more quickly, she had equipped herself with a torch and, unbeknown to either the Watch Committee, or the Chief Constable, had made herself responsible for the security of central Gorton. She worked a regular evening patrol, 7pm – 3am, seven nights a week, with no annual leave, not even the statutory bank holidays. Not being officially attested to the C Division, she hadn't been issued with a uniform, but a kindly Sergeant had given her a small pink umbrella, which not only acted as protection against the elements, but served as her badge of office. She was the only patrolwoman we had on the C and in her unstinting efforts to maintain an orderly society, she had few equals. She wasn't an interesting conversationalist but one could hardly expect a member of the Gorton Speakers Society to walk up and down Cross Street all night long, combating crime, armed only with a torch and a pink brolly.

□ □ □ □

"Fifteen two, fifteen four and one for his knobs."

Nicotine-stained fingers moved the spent matchstick along one of the rows of holes drilled into the heavy brass-topped board. The Sergeant and three constables were playing cribbage and it was the end of their refreshment break. To provide constant police cover on the division, refreshments were taken in two periods. On nights, they were taken at 1.15am and 2am. After awarding Kay an early finish and walking her partway home, I had just entered Gorton Section House for the second period. I brewed a jug of tea and sat down at the dining-room table with my sandwiches. The three card players should now return to their beats. Instead, the game dragged on to its close.

"Another game lads?" suggested the Sergeant and the three old coppers, all recruited in the 1920s, readily agreed. This night was to be no different from last night and the night before that. Although they could do little about it, many senior officers objected to the men playing cards on duty, considering it to be a misuse of time. I agreed with them, partly because it encouraged people to scrounge, but mainly because of the unpleasantness it could cause. One friendly game had almost ended in a stand-up fight.

I opened my pack of sandwiches – boiled ham again! At two in the morning my stomach wouldn't allow me to eat either cooked or spicy food. The gas fire was turned to its maximum setting and the overpowering heat in the room, coupled with the obnoxious smell of re-cycled beer fumes, mingling with the gaseous discharges from the Sergeant, who was exceedingly drunk and breaking wind at regular intervals, was enough to knock you out.

Jim, the owl man, walked into the room, saw the scroungers still playing cards, crinkled his nose in disgust, shrugged his shoulders resignedly and turned to walk back to his office. It was time something was done about it and I made my move.

"Oh, Jim," I called, "could I have a word with you?"

I followed him into the small office and winked at him. Standing in the corner was the Sergeant's stick, a four foot long, highly-polished piece of light ash. Only Inspectors and Sergeants carried such a stick and it served as an identification of their rank. I picked up the stick, mouthed the words, "Watch this", and quietly left the station.

After a few seconds, I marched briskly back in, allowing the stick to catch on the stone step with a sharp click. To every policeman the sound was unmistakable and synonymous with authority. To pre-war policemen, brought up in much harsher times, when certain of the senior officers were overbearing and spiteful in their attitudes, it was often a prelude to misfortune. After tapping the front step, I marched quickly into the dining-room and, placing the stick upright in front of me, leant on it, whilst gazing at the malingering card sharps, rather like a Vaudeville entertainer studying his audience. Jim followed me into the room and laughed out loud, for the ploy had worked perfectly. Thinking that an Inspector was about to pounce on them, each had reacted in his own way. The pack of cards was scattered like confetti and the Sergeant was hastily trying to scoop the remaining few off the table. One constable was reaching for his helmet and the other two had jumped to their feet and were buttoning their tunics. Each face registered both surprise and alarm.

I almost felt sorry for them; one small tap with a stick had practically reduced the quartet to nervous wrecks. They were doubtless recalling earlier days when dismissal from the Force was common and certain malicious Inspectors made a habit of creeping up on them in the night.

One such Inspector, a man called Pender, was alleged to have been as sympathetic and as compassionate with the workforce, as Attila the Hun with his enemies and he was universally hated. He was a despot who would stoop to the lowest tricks in his efforts to discipline officers for the most trivial offences. Years later, after his death, his name rolled off the tongues of old coppers. In the night, should a door blow open in the wind, or an unusual noise be heard, one of them would be guaranteed to look up and say, "Pender!"

The four settled back down to their game of cribbage, but it was obvious that all the enjoyment had gone out of it. Having a youngster put the wind up them had dented their self-respect and, after a short while, the Sergeant called time and put the board and cards away. The constables put on their helmets, buttoned up their tunics and went out to their beats. The Sergeant buttoned up his tunic with his back towards me – he had seen enough of me for one night. He belched uncomfortably and again broke wind. There was no doubt about it, the beer had turned sour on him. But before he left the station, he turned to glare at me and snarled.

"Tits like you we can do without."

He was obviously very upset and I decided that to say nothing was the best course of action under the circumstances.

□ □ □ □

A few weeks later, again in the early hours of the morning, I sat at the same table, preparing to eat my supper. I looked at my sandwiches – boiled ham again! Shortly after my first night duty, I had told my mother that hot or spicy food in the early hours disagreed with me and then made the mistake of telling her that boiled ham didn't. That was it, until I married, six years later, whenever I turned out for nights, there was always a pack of boiled ham sandwiches prepared for me. Being one of five brothers, I would often hear her call across the kitchen to one of the others:

"Don't touch that boiled ham, it's for Tony's supper."

After I married, I made the same mistake again, when I told my young wife I liked tomatoes. Twelve months later I had to ask her to stop giving them to me!

"Umph, you told me you liked tomatoes," she said, indignantly.

On this night, seated around the table, was a different category of men. Mainly post-war entrants, but not as young as me. The majority of men recruited after the war were ex-servicemen, many of whom had had considerable battle experience. What a wonderful atmosphere these war veterans created. They would sit around the table and their stories would start to pour out. In the still hours, the monastery at Casino would again come under attack and four thousand Polish infantrymen would be mistakenly bombed by the RAF, as they advanced against the mountain fortress. Planes would be caught and held in a cone of searchlights over Berlin; parachute lines would become entangled over Arnhem and photographs would be produced by Desert Rats, who'd been snapped whilst crouched over the sand at their ablutions. They never told lies but frequently their stories would become over-embellished and then someone would call out:

"Swing the lamp. I was sailing on the Dead Sea before it went sick."

And someone would raise an arm and knock the electric light bulb, causing it to swing to and fro, reminding them of ships ploughing through heavy seas. Those were wonderful days for the reliving of memories of the not-too-distant past.

One ex-serviceman with considerable war experience, was Jimmy the One and we were waiting for him to come in for his supper. Jim had served from 1939 until 1946 in the Submarine Service, the latter years as a First Lieutenant (Number One) at sea. He was a tall, lean, quiet man, who would listen to some of the taller stories with a straight face but smiling eyes. With a little encouragement, he would sometimes relate a story himself but the tales he told were always devoid of heroism and had the ring of truth. Old Jim, the owl man, was the one who liked to get him going and whilst the ex-submariner was telling his story, old Jim would sit absolutely enthralled, his jaw cupped in one hand, reminding me of that old painting, *The Tales of Raleigh*.

One story, which he told well, concerned his crew lying submerged outside a Norwegian fiord, waiting for the German heavy battleship, *Tirpitz*, to come out of refuge. Apparently, information had been received from intelligence sources that the *Tirpitz* was making steam and preparing to leave her berth. Jim's submarine had been detailed to wait at the mouth of the fiord and to torpedo the great battleship, should the opportunity arise.

Inside their cramped submerged craft, the men waited anxiously. It was considered to be a near suicide mission for, should the *Tirpitz* make for the open seas and the British shipping lanes, she would be heavily escorted by destroyers. Even if they managed to fire torpedoes at her, their chances of survival were slim, particularly in those icy waters.

Jim's quiet, understated delivery added to the drama of the story.

For three days and nights they waited for the *Tirpitz* to appear; 72 hours, during which the tension in the boat mounted. Then, after all, their mission was cancelled – the *Tirpitz* was no longer making steam. In the submarine there was a sigh of relief as they crept away, undetected and, later, they said their prayers.

The door opened and Jimmy the One strolled in, a quarter of an hour late for his break. The Sergeant glanced at his watch.

"You're late, Jim."

Jim nodded and came over to sit down at the table.

"Yes, I've just seen a most unusual sight, which delayed me. I'd been up to Abbey Hey to check the Co-op and was making my way in for supper, when I saw a naked man crossing the road in front of me."

The Sergeant looked up sharply.

"Naked?"

"Absolutely naked," replied Jim, "starkers."

"When was this?"

"About half an hour ago. I was about a hundred yards away from him. It's difficult to say what he was up to … dodging about in the side streets. Before I'd got within fifty yards of him, he'd spotted me and was off like a flash."

"How'd you describe him?"

"From fifty yards, at night, I could only describe him as naked," said Jim, thoughtfully, "but he seemed to know the area well. No sooner had he spotted me, than he was away, racing through the back passageways like a bloody phantom."

As Jim was telling us about the naked runner, old Jim interrupted.

"Big chap, dark hair?"

"Yes, as far as I could make out," replied Jimmy the One.

The Sergeant looked across at the old veteran.

"Any previous sightings of him?"

Old Jim, being the regular man on the section, would know the answer. "Aye, two, to the best of my knowledge, Sarge. Both about eighteen months ago and both times in the early hours of the morning."

"Any complaints from the fair sex?" asked the Sergeant.

"None at all. He's never molested anyone, or flashed it about. I think the poor beggar's simply affected by the moon."

At his point, the stalker from the highlands decided it was time to change the subject.

"You were telling me about the Tirpitz … "

The next few nights passed without incident, with me on my usual beat, patrolling up and down the streets, liaising with K11, then making my way to the station house for more tall stories, as I ate my refreshments. Nothing more had been seen of the naked man.

At 11pm one Tuesday night, I had been called to the scene of an accident, in which a man, his wife and his mother-in-law, had each been slightly injured. I was completing my report when, at 1.15am, members of the first group entered the section house for their supper. As I checked over my report, one of them casually asked:

"Bad accident?"

"No, not at all. Just three people slightly injured. Two more statements than normal. Oh! and then the driver wanted to tell me his life story. If his wife hadn't wanted to go to the toilet, I'd still be there," I joked.

"Talking about going to the toilet. Did I ever tell you about one of our officers in Normandy?"

Inadvertently having provided the cue for another story, I looked across at the speaker and noticed the two rows of campaign ribbons on his opened tunic. He had served as a tank driver in the Armoured Corps.

"Aye," he said, "it was at the back end, during the Normandy campaign. Bad tank country that. Nowt but small fields and thick hedgerows, with bloody Jerries holed up behind nearly every soddin' one of 'em. No open spaces at all in which you could get going."

He paused, as if the memory of those fields had made him lose the thread of his story.

"How does the toilet come into it?" I prompted.

"Oh, yes. Well, we had this officer, grand fella, one of the lads really. Eat with you, share a joke with you but, funnily enough, he always had to creep off miles away to have a crap in seclusion." After taking time off to attack his sandwiches, he resumed his tale. "Aye, each morning, regular as clockwork, whilst the rest of us were brewing up, he'd pick up a shovel from the tank and set off along the hedgerow, almost to the corner of the field, drop his slacks, stick his arse into the hedge, walk back, wash his hands and then come and have a cup of tea with us."

"So?" I asked.

"Well, this particular morning, the gunner decided to play a joke on him. Before the officer set off, he grabbed a spare shovel, crawled through the hedge and went along the other side of it, to the top corner of the field. When the officer came along for his morning crap, the gunner crawled up behind him, sliding the shovel silently through the hedge and positioning it under the officer's arse. He collected everything that came his way. When the officer had just about finished, the gunner withdrew the shovel and crept back down the hedgerow to join us. Meanwhile, we leant against the tank and watched him. He stood up, hooked his braces over his shoulders and then looked behind him. Baffled, he began to poke about in the hedge with his shovel, obviously wondering where it had gone. He was still looking puzzled when he came for his cup of tea. 'Everything OK, Sir?' asked the gunner. 'Everything's fine,' replied the officer. 'Oh, you looked as though you'd lost something, Sir.' 'Did I? No, no, everything's fine, thank you, Spud.'" The tank driver smiled as he reminisced. "Bloody awful days but I wouldn't have missed them for anything."

Perhaps I shouldn't generalise when discussing the merits of men, for there were many exceptions, some of them very notable. But I the difference between these two generations of policemen was very evident. The old coppers panicked at the sound of a stick being tapped on the doorstep, whilst some of these chaps wouldn't have noticed if you had exploded a bomb behind them. They were of the same breed, recruited from similar backgrounds, but one generation had been conditioned by a depression, whilst the other, even though they had been through a war, had had the advantage of seeing something of another world. In the three years after the war, much of the latter's philosophy had rubbed off on the old-timers, but it was not easy to alter the habits of years.

In the station, the Sergeant glanced at me and, anticipating that he needed to check my report, I handed it to him, then prepared to return to the beat.

I made my way out of the station and set off slowly along Hyde Road at the regulation pace. All was still and quiet, not a vehicle moving on the road and not a soul in sight. I had walked past the junction of Church Lane, when, suddenly, I saw a man's head emerge from a side passageway, some 60 yards ahead. For several seconds he gazed along Hyde Road and, as he didn't turn his head to look towards me, it seemed obvious that he was not a villain keeping 'nick', whilst his partners in crime were busily breaking and entering a nearby shop.

As I neared the passageway, I became much more alert. In anticipation of trouble, my hands came out of my pockets and I gripped the torch in my right fist. Creeping forward on tiptoe, like a fox on the prowl, I stayed close to the buildings. Suddenly the head re-appeared, looking away from me, before withdrawing again into the passage. Could this be a jealous husband awaiting the arrival of his wife and her lover, hiding in a place where he could see but not be seen? Or was it just another oddball? On the C Division there were plenty of those!

All these thoughts passed through my mind and, when I was 20 or so yards away from the alley, I saw the head pop out yet again, completely unaware of my silent approach.

My arrival at the end of the alleyway coincided with yet another re-appearance and I do not honestly know who was the more surprised. From a distance of four feet I was staring at a naked man – it was the runner. As I was in night uniform, which was equipped with black buttons, black helmet badge and cone flashings, he must have thought that he was looking at the Man in Black.

For what seemed like an eternity, but could not have been more than a second or two, we stared at each other in amazement. Suddenly he turned and fled, with me close behind him, in a scene reminiscent of the Keystone Cops. But, having been a schoolboy sprint champion, I had the advantage. However, as he had no clothes on, I found it difficult to catch hold of him as, surprisingly, he was greasy with sweat.

I chased him through several passageways, grabbing at him whenever I drew level, but each time I grabbed, I lost momentum and somehow or other he would slip through my grasp, leaving me watching his buttocks, churning away five yards in front of me. I finally brought the chase to an end by bringing him down from behind in a sliding football tackle and then dived on top of his prostrate form with my full weight. If a referee had been present, he would have certainly blown his whistle for a foul, but in that situation, what else could I do?

It is a bad time in a policeman's life when he realises that he is tangling with someone who is stronger than himself and this was a new experience for me. As I grasped his upper arm, I found, with a nasty shock, that I had hold of good hard muscle. Lying on top of a naked man, in a back entry, in the early hours of the morning, was bad enough, but to find that he was both fit and muscular was too much. As we lay there panting, it was like music to my ears when he said:

"OK. I'm glad you've caught me. I'll be no trouble."

Getting to our feet and staring at each other in the darkness, we waited to catch our breath. Then we walked back along the passageways and I picked up my cape, which I had dropped in the chase. I handed it to him to wrap round himself, whilst I escorted him to the section house.

He was a nice man, some ten years older than myself. He told me he was a blacksmith's striker and had served most of the war years in the Fourteenth Army in Burma. His naked nocturnal wanderings had started shortly after his demobilisation and he could not explain why, or how, they had come about. I escorted him home and enlightened his wife, to some extent, about what had been happening and collected his clothing from where he had left it, in their outside toilet. Then, accompanied by his wife, I took him to the Manchester Royal Infirmary, where he was treated as an out-patient. There were no more sightings of the naked runner.

Five years later, one Sunday morning, I met him again, when he was out walking with his young daughter. I was prepared to nod to him and walk past but was more than a little pleased when he stopped to chat. We spoke, as all Englishmen do, about the weather and football. It was the time of the Busby Babes, so we had much we talk about.

Footprints in the Snow – 25 Beat

When parading for duty, I would make certain initial entries in my pocket notebook such as the date, Mode of Working, lighting-up time and anything which required my attention. Then, when retiring from duty, say on 25 Beat, on the afternoon relief, I would either endorse the notebook – 'Retired 10pm Mill Street. No reports' – and sign the entry, or, if I had been required to submit written reports, make a note accordingly.

To the inexperienced eye, the endorsement – 'No reports' – might suggest that the tour of duty had been uneventful but that was not necessarily so. I can recall four completely different incidents which, whilst not in themselves significant enough to warrant a written report, have remained locked in my memory with every detail as crystal clear as if they had happened yesterday

One of the more unpleasant aspects of policework is that of dealing with people suffering from mental illness for, as part of their duty, Police Officers are required to take into custody any person who, in a public place, appears to be suffering from a mental disorder and needs immediate care and control. That person would then be taken to a place of safety and detained for up to 72 hours, whilst he is examined by a doctor and interviewed by a Mental Welfare Officer.

Prior to 1959, the Mental Welfare Officer was known as the Relieving Officer and patients were often removed from their homes under what was known as a Three Day Order. Usually, acting on information from a patient's family, the Relieving Officer, after first satisfying himself that it was necessary, would obtain this order and remove the patient, whilst he arranged for him to be medically examined. It was a sad but necessary business and when putting the order into effect, the Relieving Officer frequently sought the assistance of a Police Officer.

Having had a couple of unpleasant experiences involving mentally disturbed people, I wasn't exactly euphoric when, one Saturday morning, a middle-aged Relieving Officer drew his car alongside me, as I was patrolling 25 Beat. After identifying himself, he asked me to accompany him to a nearby house, where a young man had become mentally unbalanced and was behaving in a most abnormal manner, growling and barking at people and, to make matters worse, biting them whenever possible.

I got into the car and noted, with some trepidation, that the official was puffing nervously at a cigarette and seemed preoccupied with his thoughts, as if anticipating trouble.

"I'm sorry to bother you, Officer," he apologised, whilst staring straight ahead, "but things could get a little out of hand. I know you must be a busy chap but I'll try to deal with it as quickly as possible."

That was all he had time to say for, seconds later, he pulled up outside a neat mid-terrace house, in a pleasant part of the neighbourhood.

"I'll go in on my own," he suggested, "then, if I need your assistance, I'll come out for you."

He entered the house without closing the door behind him and, a few seconds later, hurried out again.

"Perhaps you'd better come along with me, Officer. The patient appears to be rather aggressively disposed."

Following him into the lounge, we encountered a young man, trembling violently, with bared teeth. He was of athletic build, naked to the waist and flanked by his parents, who were trying to comfort him, as he stared about with bulging eyes. The Relieving Officer spoke to him gently, attempting to persuade him to accompany us but without the desired effect for, when he moved towards him, the young man backed away and started to growl menacingly. The Relieving Officer caught him ineffectively by the arm and the young man easily shrugged him off, then leapt over the settee and rushed upstairs. The job had become ten times more difficult, for now, we not only had to overpower him, but we also had to manhandle him down a narrow staircase.

I moved cautiously up the stairs and entered the rear bedroom, where the young man was sheltering behind his younger brother, who stood weeping by the bed. I was quite unprepared for this emotional scene and being of a similar age and one of five brothers myself, my heart immediately went out to both of them.

The patient turned to me and started to shout, as if to to a dog.

"Cease! Cease! Do you hear me? Cease!"

It was nerve-racking and distressing.

Still sobbing, the patient's brother left the room at the request of the Relieving Officer and went to join his parents downstairs. There followed a terrific struggle, in which the patient and I rolled down the stairs, almost from top to bottom. Once there, he started to weep and fell silent. Whilst his parents were assisting him to dress, he became rational and started to appeal to his brother for help. It was heart-rending. Once inside the car, he sat quietly between his father and brother on the rear seat, staring straight ahead and was driven away peacefully, allowing me to return to my beat.

Later, at Mill Street Station, the Inspector called me to one side.

"The Relieving Officer's been on the phone (it was customary for them to thank officers, through official channels, for assistance rendered) and from what he was telling me, you've had one hell of a job. Well done."

I looked at him with a lump in my throat.

"To be honest with you, Sir, there was nothing well done about that job at all, it was simply awful."

He saw how it had affected me and tried to cheer me up.

"Don't let it get you down, Ninety-six. It's all in a day's work."

I nodded glumly but said nothing, not entirely convinced that it should be.

The Inspector was a keen Manchester United supporter and we had often discussed football. He had soon discovered where my allegiance lay.

"Go and watch Stockport County this afternoon, they're playing Crewe. Now if you are genuinely interested in good football, that's something you will find really heartbreaking."

I couldn't help but smile. When talking football with him I should have been more discreet, particularly about the merits of my home team.

He winked at me.

"Good lad, and just remember, Ninety-six, you're too young to carry the worries of this world on your shoulders."

□ □ □ □

I had paraded at Divisional Headquarters for night duty, thoroughly fed-up and feeling out of sorts. The station made an appropriate backdrop to my mood – a depressingly ugly Victorian edifice, built to withstand a siege, it did nothing to dispel my gloom. Earlier in the evening, I had been out on a date which had gone wrong and, not for the first time, I had been given the elbow. After quickly changing into uniform, I had left home in a rush and, to make matters worse, had forgotten to bring along either my torch, or my sandwiches. It was going to be one of those nights!

After parading, I walked along a draughty, green-tiled corridor to draw a beat lamp at the charge office. I made my request and was directed to the cobbled yard, where a knob stick clerk was testing the antiquated lamps against the wall of the cycle shed. He had collected them from the afternoon relief and was now checking them before they were reissued to the men on night duty. He stood about six yards away from the wooden shed, pointed a lamp at it and then switched on the beam. If the beam reached the shed, the lamp was issued immediately, if it didn't, he would give it a second chance, by moving a good yard or two closer and trying again. Only if it failed this test, would he consider issuing a new battery. It was a time of austerity everywhere in Great Britain and, on the C Division, even light was rationed. But most of the young constables provided their own torches, whilst many of the older officers only needed to find their way to the pubs!

The lamp I drew failed the first test, but passed the second. In disgust, I hooked it into the buttonhole of my greatcoat and set out into the night, utterly depressed. It was late October, murky, with a touch of drizzle in the air, which turned to heavier rain as I headed towards my beat along Ashton Old Road. I flung my cape around me and, without buttoning it up, clipped it round my neck with the brass chain. It was too warm for both cape and greatcoat but, until I arrived at a police box, I would just have to suffer!

I reached 25 Beat and started to shake hands with the door handles of the main road shops. In the distance, the light on top of the police box was flashing. I hastened towards it, disposed of my heavy greatcoat and answered the telephone. It was a 'domestic'. The operator warned me that there was a disturbed woman out there, sending out distress signals with a voice like a fog-horn.

I made my way to a large, semi-detached house about a mile away and knocked on the front door. A large, bony, middle-aged lady answered and invited me in. I followed her into the kitchen and saw that she had been weeping. Unlike the scene of many domestic disturbances, the house was well decorated, spotlessly clean and well furnished. The woman promptly burst into tears.

"It's him, Officer, he's been at it again. My breasts are black and blue with him," she boomed.

The house may have been different, but the story was the same.

"It seems all quiet now," I ventured. "Perhaps if you both went to bed and slept it off, maybe that would be the best thing."

She wasn't the type to be put off so easily and she went to the foot of the stairs and yelled aloft:

"You're a different person now the policeman's here, aren't you?" She paused. When there was no reply she began again. "Different when there's a man here, isn't it? Fit for nothing else than bullying helpless women, you are."

She would have been the ideal sort of person to have by you in an armed hostage situation, when you needed to speak to the kidnappers without being seen. Following her tirade, she returned to the kitchen and, after counselling her for a few seconds, I was preparing to leave. Once a domestic had settled down, I had learnt not to delay departing the scene, before it started up again.

Suddenly, standing belligerently in the frame of the kitchen door, as if determined to make his presence felt, was 'him from upstairs', a mere bantam of a man. He was balding with a small ginger moustache and was smartly attired in navy blue pin-striped trousers and waistcoat, complemented by a stiff, white-collared shirt and a blue, polka dot tie. He didn't speak, but simply stared at me, assessing the situation. I gained the impression that he had dealt with men far more experienced than myself and wondered what was coming my way.

"Just a moment," he said haughtily, then disappeared back into the hallway. A few seconds later he was back. He'd put on his suit jacket and a black bowler hat. Now dressed for the part, he pointed at me and sharply clicked his thumb and forefinger together. "You! Out! Out of my house immediately! I'm the householder here and you're not here at my invitation."

I nodded to him. His timing had been out by 30 seconds. I hadn't been in the Force long but I had already had the benefit of dozens of such encounters. One thing I couldn't allow was to be ordered away from the scene of a domestic, not even one which seconds earlier I was eagerly preparing to leave.

"Fine by me," I replied.

He didn't merely accompany me, as with an invited guest, he strode quickly in front, flung open the door and pointed into the street.

"Out," he commanded.

It was a bleak, wet night. Closing the kitchen door behind me, I pushed the front door to and stood facing him, or rather, looking down on him. Having explained to him the embarrassment that such an exit would cause me, so early in my career, he looked up at me from under the rim of his bowler hat and started to cry.

"It's her, Officer. She's got a sharp tongue and never gives me a moment's peace."

Startled by this dramatic change in attitude, I left with the usual message delivered on such occasions:

"Well, there'll be trouble if I have to come back tonight."

Two hours later and still patrolling the beat in the pouring rain, I began to think about supper. Not that I ever enjoyed my food in the middle of the night. In any case I had left my sandwiches at home. I was just looking forward to a few friendly faces and a chat.

In the three hours I had been on duty, I would normally have been visited by the Section Sergeant but Paddy was on duty that night. The inclement weather and the number of pubs between Mill Street and 25 Beat didn't help matters. He would wait at the section house until I showed up for my refreshments and then expect me to 'show him a flyer'. This meant me making a false entry in my notebook recording a visit by the Sergeant – a common practice in the C Division.

Still thinking about a break, I turned off the main road and entered a narrow passageway leading to the rear of a row of lock-up shops. The weather had deteriorated even further and now, flashes of lightning forked across the sky and there were loud claps of thunder overhead. I turned sharply into a covered ginnel (a roofed passageway). Here the walls were so close together that my shoulders brushed them as I walked along with my cape wrapped firmly around me. By this stage, the battery in my lamp was virtually exhausted and could barely produce a glimmer of light.

Four feet above my head, the arched roof prevented even the night light from penetrating the darkness. It was ink black but at least it was dry and the only sounds to be heard were my footsteps echoing in the confined space. My mind was almost a blank when, suddenly, my helmet and face bumped into something which swung away from me, then back, like a pendulum, to again brush against me. I stopped in my tracks, dived with my right hand for my beat lamp and slammed my left hand out in front of me, groping about in the darkness at face level. Momentarily, I touched something that shouldn't have been there – it felt like a pair of shoes – but whatever it was swung away from my touch before I could be certain. Switching on the clumsy beat lamp, my left hand again made contact with something and, this time, I was able to catch hold of it. Not shoes, but boots and, higher up, I could now feel a pair of trousers. I hadn't realised I had been holding my breath but just managed to utter two swear words before gulping for air.

Out of the weak glimmer of light, emerged the form of a man, suspended by his neck, swinging gently to and fro at the end of a short length of rope, attached to an overhead beam. The hair rose on the back of my neck and I felt my knees begin to buckle. In the early hours of the morning I was quite unprepared for the shock of this gruesome discovery and had to steady myself and recover somewhat, by pressing my back against the ginnel wall, then crouching down, so that I could breathe more freely. A jumble of thoughts raced through my mind. Who was he? Had he committed suicide? Why?

I knew what I had to do – cut him down and make certain that he was dead. But first I had to get a grip on myself. In the dim light, his face looked cadaverous and grotesque – like a deformed death mask. From six feet away I couldn't really make it out. I caught hold of the trousers and stopped the body from swaying. Standing on tiptoe, I raised my right hand and shone the lamp directly into his face, from a distance of a few inches. On closer inspection it was even more horrific – eye sockets but no eyes, wide gaping mouth but no teeth, yellow, parchment-like skin. The face was indeed unnatural and masklike. I pushed the whole thing away from me in disgust and relief! Closer inspection had revealed it to be nothing more than a Guy Fawkes! It was unthinkable to tell my colleagues that a Guy Fawkes had just given me the fright of my life and I didn't try, but back at Mill Street, I vented my wrath on the knobstick clerk who had issued the faulty beat lamps, calling him all the names I could put my tongue to.

☐ ☐ ☐ ☐

In 1949 a policeman had to know his beat and he had to know it well. This can't be claimed for the modern policeman, as the system no longer allows it. To obtain this knowledge, the conscientious city bobby had to spend eight hours a day, six days a week, on foot patrol. Having walked down every street on the patch, spoken to many of its inhabitants and taken the children across the school-crossing points four times a day, then, and only then, would he begin to get the feel of things.

Nor was it a matter of walking about, head in the clouds. Irregularities were noted on the surface of the footpaths and the Highways Department informed; gas escapes were detected, as was water running to waste and the appropriate authorities notified. Because there was a constant police presence, motor vehicles were rarely left in dangerous positions on the roads and, although there were many cases of obstruction, one rarely saw a vehicle parked on the footpath. At least 95% of cars had current excise licences, even if the occasional fly-boy tried it on with the odd Guinness label in its place. In the late evening, gangs of youths were never allowed to congregate on footpaths, nor were drunks allowed to obstruct the doors of public houses. They were moved on and often none too politely.

At night, the beatman had to become acquainted with all the lock-up property. It was expected that he check it twice nightly – back and front – and any insecurity, or unusual light, reported. It was tedious work, but it was effective. The system was abandoned with the arrival of the Panda car. The job became easier but at the public's expense. After a year or two of driving about in a car, not only did the bobby lose touch with the local people but also became reluctant to leave his vehicle.

If you ask a retired C Division man what he remembered about the back entries, he would probably reply, "the cat shit". There seemed to be acres of it waiting to be stepped on. Apart from that, they were remarkably free of rubbish and generally cleaner than most main roads are today.

Ever since I was a child, I have loved snow and still do. Snow falling at night could be a great help to the beatman. Not only did the city appear cleaner, lighter and brighter but, after initially checking his area, further examination was often unnecessary – a quick glance down a passageway would reveal whether another set of footprints had appeared since his last visit.

Later in the year, on 25 Beat, on just such a winter's night, I was checking property at the rear of Ashton Old Road and everything was covered in a blanket of white snow. I arrived at the end of a passageway, behind a row of shops and, much to my surprise, noticed that someone had been there already. Leading down the carpet of otherwise virgin snow, was a neat set of footprints, which ended 15 yards along the passageway, at its junction with another passage. Who had turned into that second passageway, and was he still there? I soon discounted the theory that it was the Sergeant or Inspector checking up on me, as I couldn't imagine either of them wanting to play such a dirty trick.

There was only one way to find out. Creeping along the entry, keeping close to the left hand wall, I pressed each foot down slowly, to minimise the sound of crunching snow. Nearing the end of the trail, I stopped and held my breath, to listen carefully. I could hear the sound of heavy breathing; someone was waiting for me around the corner of the second passageway. Instinctively I knew that it was not a courting couple, besides ,there had only been one set of footprints. I froze against the wall and continued to listen. I could still hear the sound of heavy breathing. Whoever it was appeared to be waiting. I drew my staff and inched slowly forwards until I was almost level with the entrance to the passageway. Tensing myself, I switched on my torch and launched myself round the corner. Four feet away, a very overweight man was sitting on the step of a house gate. He had taken one shoe and sock off and was sitting in six inches of snow, picking intently at his foot to remove a corn! Every time he leant forward, he pressed his belly against his knees and gasped out a cloud of beery fumes.

"Do you know what time it is?" I managed to ask.

"Aye, it's just after midnight, Officer."

He was so drunk he thought I was actually asking him the time because I needed to know! And he carried on attending to his feet, as if he was in the privacy of his own front room.

On Christmas Day in the Morning – 13 Beat

It was my second Christmas on C Division and Christmas Day coincided with a quick changeover of duties. Thus, I was required to finish a shift at 10pm on Christmas Eve and report back for duty at 6am the following morning. As if that in itself wasn't bad enough, there was no public transport early on Christmas morning, so it was a job for the bike – six miles on the old boneshaker over cobbled roads. If that didn't wake me up, nothing would!

At home, my brothers had arranged for a party to be held on Christmas Eve and, at 21 years of age, sleep or no sleep, I wasn't going to miss it. The party was a lively affair and at 4am I decided that there was little point in going to bed and settled down to a few more light ales. At 5am I clambered unsteadily into my uniform, experiencing more than a little difficulty getting into the trousers, donned my helmet and greatcoat, pushed the big roadster out into the roadway, looped my folded cape over the handlebars and was finally given a cheery, power-assisted start by two brothers. I took a deep gulp of the freezing air and with a final wave, set off on my journey over the cobbled roads, in a less than sober state.

There was not a soul to be seen, or a sound to be heard, save for that of my tyres skimming over the icy setts. The moon was shining brightly, casting its glow over the hilly town and causing the frost on the rooftops to glisten and sparkle. But, as I gripped the handlebars, which were vibrating like a pneumatic drill, I was more aware of the cold and the effect it was having on my fingers, which I could feel tingling painfully, despite wearing two pairs of gloves.

The first two miles were the easiest, travelling downhill with scarcely a need to touch the pedals, except for a quick burst or two to keep up the momentum. Into the centre of Stockport I rode, without even the need to draw a deep breath. Then came the hard bit – a long hill leading upwards and outwards to Manchester. I raced towards it at maximum speed, then began to lose momentum as the gradient began to take effect. Halfway up and the sweat-band of my helmet was soaked in sweat, as I swayed from side to side in my effort to keep going. Before reaching the top I had left the saddle and was standing on the pedals like a Tour de France cyclist, passing through the Pyrenees. Puffing and grunting but visibly wilting with every passing second until, finally, I reached the crest of the hill with a sigh of relief.

After that hill, the next four miles were quite easy and I settled down to some relaxed pedalling. I finally arrived at my destination, vaulted stylishly off the bike, pushed it through the iron gates and onto the cycle rack, removed the steel spring clips from around my ankles and walked into Levenshulme Section House. Paddy wasn't on duty and Bill Collard, a first-class old copper, was in charge.

"Morning, Bill, Merry Christmas."

I went to shake his hand.

"Oh, Merry Christmas, Ninety-six. You look as fresh as a daisy this morning."

I thought, at first, that he was joking but he was serious. I'd had no sleep for 24 hours, wasn't sober, was sweating like a bull and was well and truly bushed. It's amazing what you can get away with when you're only 21 and have a fresh and rosy complexion!

I entered the small parade room cum dining-room, placed my staff, snaps and notebook on the table, removed my helmet and sat down. Bill glanced at my appointments.

"You can put those away," he smiled cheerfully. "There'll be no parade this morning," and he turned to pick up the duty roster. "There's only you and me and Reuben on duty in Levenshulme until two o'clock." What he next said was most unexpected. "There'll be no working the beat this morning. It's Christmas out there and it's also Christmas in here. Take your greatcoat off, hang your helmet up, put the kettle on and when you've done that, relax."

It was the first time in 16 months that someone had told me to relax and he couldn't have chosen a better time.

"Where's Reuben?" I asked.

Bill Collard smiled.

"He was VLP last night." The smile changed to a broad grin and then to a chuckle. "VLP on a Christmas Eve. Who could ask – for more?" He glanced at his watch. "We can give him another half hour or so before we need to worry about him," then added, thoughtfully, "at this moment he's probably too drunk to stand upright."

VLP – Visiting Licensed Premises – was one of the prime duties on C Division and one for which the young constables didn't qualify. It was considered, by those who published the duty roster, to be one of the perks of long service and, as such, was jealously guarded. It was an official, eight hour tour of duty, cum pub crawl. It started at 5.30pm each Friday and Saturday evening and lasted until the Sergeant and constable allocated the tour had had enough. Or, if Paddy of the ill-fitting teeth was the Sergeant, until someone went out to fetch him in.

It was some years later in my service before I was selected to perform this particular weekend task and, on that occasion, a Sergeant and I paraded at Mill Street Station at 5pm on the Friday evening. By 5.30pm we were at the top of Ashton Old Road, Higher Openshaw, close to the city boundary and ready for action. During the next eight hours, we made our way down the road, calling in at every pub, until we reached the heart of Ancoats. The purpose of our visits was to check that all the licensed premises were kept clean, run in an orderly manner and the conditions of the licence observed. During my time on C Division, these visits seemed to have lost their purpose, for it is fair to say there were few, if any, disorderly houses.

For those selected to visit licensed premises, the modus operandi was simple, but one which was well adhered to. The police visitors would walk through the pub door where, the bush telegraph being what it was, they would be greeted by the landlord and his wife. Each would enquire about the other's health and then the Sergeant would compliment the landlady, often in the most flattering terms. She would respond by inviting the visitors into their living quarters, where they would be offered a drink. Sometimes it would be refused, in which case a packet of cigarettes would be offered. In many of the pubs, both cigarettes and a drink would be proffered and human nature being what it is, both would be accepted.

Somewhere on the route an Inspector who, having allocated the duty in the first place, would intercept them and be given 40 cigarettes. At any time between 1am and 3am, the VLP party would retire from duty, usually the worse for wear, with every pocket bulging with cigarettes. If the acceptance of these gifts was a form of bribery, I honestly never saw the reason why. During my time on the division, I saw few people engaged in under-age drinking and in most pubs the atmosphere was jovial, with no unseemly behaviour. In bestowing their favours, it was as if the licensees were honouring what had become an acknowledged local custom.

In the section house we had finished our jug of tea and were patiently awaiting the arrival of Reuben, who was already more than half an hour late. Understandably, considering that he had mixed VLP with the traditional Christmas Eve celebrations and had had a quick changeover of duties to boot.

Bill Collard again glanced at his watch – he was getting anxious now because he had already announced to Divisional Headquarters that Reuben was on duty. He was probably wondering whether or not he had even reached home from the night before!

"You'd better go and dig him out of bed," he said to me.

Within minutes of receiving my instructions to relax, the orders were being changed! I groaned softly. Reuben lived in my own borough of Stockport, much closer to the Manchester boundary, but still three and a half miles away. It was 1949 and Reuben had no such luxury as a telephone. To get him out of bed meant remounting the boneshaker and pedalling back along those cobbled streets for three and a half miles, then knocking on his front door hard enough to arouse him.

I reached for my helmet and greatcoat and snapped the steel cycle clips around my ankles.

"OK, Bill, I'm off."

As I expected, when I arrived at his home, I found it in darkness. I knocked loud and often, knowing that Reuben lived alone. He was an old copper who had, during the latter part of the war, served in the Forces in Germany. At the close of hostilities, because of his police experience, he had been invited to remain behind to serve with the Control Commission, which had been set up to regulate events in a vanquished and divided Germany. He had been happy to oblige and, knowing him, I'm sure he enjoyed himself immensely. When he decided it was time to go home, he found that he had left it too late, for his wife was ensconced with her lover and, worse still, if police rumour was to be believed, had made off with most of Reuben's nest-egg.

From the front garden of his home, I showered gravel at the bedroom window, hammered the door with the knocker and then shouted through the letterbox. Eventually, a bedraggled Reuben opened the door and let me in. It had been easier than I expected, for he hadn't been in bed long enough to have fallen into a really deep sleep and he didn't appear to have a hangover, which prompted me to enquire how he was feeling. He reflected for a moment or two before answering.

"OK ..." There was a longer pause as he sought to gather his wits together. "... alright really. Not too bad at all, considering what I supped last night. I just feel pleasantly pissed."

He shook his head and blinked his eyes, as if trying to remember what day it was. I helped him along the way to recovery by wishing him a merry Christmas and reminding him that he was late. He blinked his eyes again and started to laugh.

"Oh, aye, it's Christmas Day, isn't it? We're on mornings." I nodded. "Who's on?" he asked.

"Just me, you and Bill Collard. Bill's sent me," I replied.

"Sergeant or Inspector there?" I shook my head. "Have I been missed?" I again shook my head.

"Not by anyone that matters."

Strewn about the lounge was the evidence of his VLP duty; packets of cigarettes lying where they had landed when he'd emptied his pockets.

"Sit down for a minute. Do you want a drink?"

"No thanks," I replied, "I've had enough to float a battleship."

He threw me 40 cigarettes.

"Have a smoke then."

Stashing the cigarettes in my pocket, I made as if to leave.

"What time is it?" he asked vaguely.

"Five past seven."

"Any buses running?"

"Not this early."

"Oh, God," he groaned, grasping his head as if it had just started to throb, "I've no transport."

Even fewer people possessed cars than telephones and Reuben didn't even possess a bike.

"Can you give me a lift?" he asked, pitifully.

I stared at him in disbelief.

"What, on the crossbar?"

"Only way I can get in."

"Come off it," I laughed, "I've already cycled ten miles over those blasted cobbles. I've just about had it." I looked across to where the two top buttons of his fly were gaping open to form a V across his large belly. "Besides which, if you sat on the crossbar, it's doubtful whether I'd be able to reach the handlebars. It's a fair old gut you've got there, Reuben."

He looked across at my meagre 13 stone frame and attempted to suck his belly into his chest before making an even more foolish suggestion.

"Well, you sit on the crossbar and I'll peddle you in."

It was still dark outside, the roads were deserted, it was Christmas. Could the bike take it? More to the point, could I take it? I studied Reuben's four chins and his 17 stone bulk.

"OK," I agreed, reluctantly, "but you pedal."

I should have had more sense. He started to put on his uniform, grunting loudly as he sat on the settee and bent forward to lace up his boots. He donned his greatcoat and helmet, placed 40 cigarettes in his pocket for Bill Collard, wrapped his refreshments into the folds of his cape and handed it to me, drew in his stomach and announced cheerfully:

"Ready when you are!"

Outside, he positioned himself astride my bike with both feet resting on the ground, whilst I balanced myself on the crossbar. At this stage, I was sober enough to realise what I was doing, but drunk enough not to care. On the other hand, Reuben, now that the fresh air had got to him, was as drunk as a lord.

"We're off!" he grunted, standing on the pedals to gain extra leverage and power.

Having done a bit of cycling in his younger days, he was really impressive for several yards, but we hadn't got to the top of his avenue before he was panting heavily and by the time we had reached the A6, he was gasping and wheezing. He pedalled laboriously along in the direction of the Manchester boundary and along that half mile stretch of road, I thought he was about to die. A more sober and compassionate man would have relinquished his position on the crossbar and taken to the pedals. Instead, I sat there and listened. His laboured breathing was accompanied by a loud strangulated sucking sound made by his mouth which, in turn, was coupled with a sniffling suffocating sound, as he tried to draw in air through his stuffed up nostrils. When he expelled air it was with a loud nerve-wracking, "phrooogh," as if his lungs had suddenly exploded. In addition to all this, the beer swilling about in his belly was making a series of orchestrated sounds, as though someone down there was performing an underwater ballet. As we neared the boundary, he managed to utter an exasperated, "I'm knackered," through the pain.

Emerging from a road on our right and turning across our path, intending to travel in our direction, was a fully-laden milk float. The milkman had just left the nearby dairy and was heading for his morning round. Reuben saw the float as his salvation. Drawing on his remaining supply of energy, he managed to pedal the 30 yards needed to draw level with it.

"Grab hold of the back of it," he belched out fiercely.

I twisted round on the crossbar, stuck out my left hand and managed to catch hold of the offside rear post, connecting the platform to the roof. All this was executed before the float had completed its right-hand turn. Suddenly, our combined weight caused the float's two nearside wheels to leave the road and the milk crates to shift with a terrifying creak. For what seemed like minutes, the milk float was suspended at an angle, until the two wheels thudded back to the ground and almost brought it to a stop. I heard the driver cry out in alarm as he thrust his head out of the cab window, in an effort to discover what sort of catastrophe had befallen him. In the dim light, he made out two policemen on a bicycle, clinging onto his float! Somehow, despite the near disaster, I managed to keep my wits about me.

"Keep moving," I shouted, in a commanding voice, "this is an emergency."

In the circumstances, the milkman's actions were highly commendable. He behaved as if it was perfectly normal practice for two Manchester Police Officers to attend emergency calls on a float-drawn bicycle. He pulled the peak of his cap low over his eyes, hunched over the steering wheel and proceeded to coax the maximum 15mph out of his float by talking to it in the most endearing terms.

"Come on now, my sweetheart."

Confident that his heart was holding out and that he wasn't going to die after all, Reuben closed his eyes and rested, allowing me to steer the cycle with my free hand. Suddenly, in his drunken state, he began to giggle, spasmodically at first, but gradually laughing more loudly and uncontrollably, barely pausing to draw breath. It wasn't long before I joined in.

"Ask him how far he's going," Reuben called out, anxious in case he had to take to the pedals again.

I transferred the enquiry to the driver.

"Midway," he called back, referring to the large mock Tudor public house which stood less than 100 yards from our destination. "Is that OK, Officer?"

"Fine," I called back.

Reuben relaxed completely, dissolving into drunken laughter and cackling away until he was nearly in hysterics. Holding onto the milkfloat with my left hand and steering the bike with my right, whilst perched on the crossbar, was no easy matter and I had to confine myself to the occasional titter.

"Midway," announced the milkman, pointing ahead by pushing his right arm through the cab window and making a flicking motion with his forefinger. "I'll slow down and let you overtake me."

As he neared the large black and white pub, he pulled into the nearside kerb and, at the same time, I let go of the float and went careering past him, wishing him a Merry Christmas as we swerved past his cab.

"Merry Christmas, Officer," he called back, "glad to have been of assistance."

I pointed the iron-framed bike in the direction of the section house sign and we slewed across the deserted road at an angle. As we approached, Reuben grabbed hold of the handlebars and tried to apply the brakes.

"They're stuck!" he yelled at the top of his voice. His folded cape had become trapped between the handlebars and the brake levers. "They're jammed, I can't stop it!"

His wild shouts and laughter brought Bill Collard to the section house door to stare at us in amazement. I was too far gone to care. We skidded across the frozen cobbles towards the section house, hit the kerb in front of it and rolled off the machine and into the gutter, where we lay helpless, laughing so much that we were unable to stand. Bill Collard stood over us with a wide smile on his face.

"Come inside you bonnie pair of beggars, before anyone else sees you."

After that, the morning went as Bill had predicted, for it was Christmas inside the station, as it was outside. For the next seven hours we sat and relaxed, waiting for calls that never came and chatting amongst ourselves.

Bring on the clowns – 17 Beat

Hollywood had a lot to answer for, certainly as far as Manchester criminals were concerned. How they must have marvelled as they sat in the darkened cinema and watched stuntmen leap across roofs, jump down flights of steps, sword in hand, fence when they got to the bottom, then be driven back up by a horde of antagonists, before hopping over the battlements into the moat. Heroes jumped through plate-glass windows to escape their enemies. Men crashed their cars at a 100 miles an hour and walked casually away from the wreck. It was all made to look so easy and no one ever got hurt.

I remember one winter's night when, along with a number of other officers, we surrounded a lock-up draper's shop in Ancoats. The burglar alarm had been activated and, suspecting that a thief was still on the premises, we had sent for the keys. Suddenly, a first floor window burst into a thousand pieces, as a figure came hurtling out of it. I spun round to be confronted by the silhouette of a man against the night sky, who appeared to be running whilst his feet were still ten feet above the ground. He seemed well positioned to land on his feet and race away like an Olympic sprinter. But he fell heavily, screamed loudly, picked himself up as if to run and then collapsed. When we went to pick him up, we found that he not only had a broken leg, but was also badly cut and his clothing was torn to shreds.

More recently, a prisoner who was being interviewed in a CID office, for no other reason than to escape, apparently leapt straight through the first floor window. He was even more unfortunate and landed on the spiked railings below.

It wasn't only the stuntmen to blame – the actors had a lot to answer for too. It is easy to remember how Cagney, Bogart and Edward G Robinson handled those big American detectives. These three were only small men and yet the way they spoke to the big powerful lawmen, you would certainly have expected them to get a boot up their backsides in return. But, no, they got away with the wisecracks, the grimaces and the thumb poked into the detective's waistcoated chest.

There's no doubt that Bernard had seen most of the gangster films – but first let me tell you about Bernard. Late one night I was strolling across the car park of the Levenshulme Palais, a dance hall of some local fame. I was with an older policeman who enjoyed the nickname of Alibi Alf. The dancing at the Palais had long finished and the band and their following had made their way home, leaving the car park almost deserted. It was a pleasant night, warm and quiet, and the last thing we were thinking about was villains.

As we walked between a car and a lorry, I heard a trickling sound and, on investigation, found that, close to the petrol tank of the lorry, was a five gallon jerrycan and connecting the two, was a length of rubber tubing. I felt the car's radiator and it was warm. I checked the number and, sure enough, it had been stolen. We looked around but there was no sign whatsoever of the milkmaid. The only explanation was that she, or indeed, he, was hiding some 30 yards away, in a brick-built air raid shelter, a relic of the war years.

We were walking towards it, when two figures dashed out of one of the entrances and had enough experience to run in different directions. I chased one and Alibi chased the other. Mine, the smaller of the two, beat me hands down and made it to the main railway line connecting Manchester with London. When I last saw him, he was in the middle of the track, heading south towards the metropolis, looking capable of overtaking the night express out of Piccadilly. I returned to Levenshulme Section House and was pleased to see that Alfie had caught the other, a big strapping 19-year-old, misguided enough to have in his pocket a big bunch of ignition keys and three log books relating to different vehicles.

We laid the contents of his pockets on the table and started to question him. We needed to know four things – who he was, where he lived, who he had been with and what illegal things he had been up to – reasonable requests in the circumstances. Now, Bernard – we did discover his name – had obviously seen all the gangster films. His voice was a combination of Cagney's and Edward G's, his facial expressions were definitely Bogart's and even included the little snicker of the top lip. In the finest Hollywood tradition, he was, "sayin' nuttin', not nohow, sucker". He obviously thought he was a real hard case.

"Get out o' me hair, bluebottle."

Now the Judges' Rules may well have been formulated to protect the likes of Bernard and even more vicious criminals, from successful interrogation. In these circumstances, the prisoner was supposed to be given the caution, *'You are not obliged to say anything unless you wish to do so, but whatever you say will be taken down in writing and may be given in evidence,'* and then the officer was expected to abide by the outcome. Policemen on C Division tended to ignore the judicial advice in relation to the official caution and, in the wider interests of crime detection, applied the Ancoats Caution. In other words, they gave the prisoner a good hiding and then asked all the relevant questions under threat of another.

Bernard's top lip was working overtime, like that of a rabbit.

"There's no need to worry about me squawking, flatfoot."

However, when I gave him my Joe Louis impression, he suddenly changed his mind and began to protest in a strong Mancunian accent.

"Eee, you can cut that out. I've had enough of that in Borstal. Alright, I'll tell you what you want to know."

Bernard was decidedly sulky but once he'd finished with his character studies, he told us what we needed to know; his name, the name of his 31-year-old associate (Jacky …) and that they were living in a drum (a poorly furnished bedsitter) in Higher Temple Street, Chorlton-on-Medlock, with Jacky's moll, a Glaswegian named Sadie.

Armed with Bernard's key, Alibi and I went down to the common lodging house in Higher Temple Street. Not wishing to disturb anyone and hoping to trap Jacky, we quietly let ourselves into the room. It was typical of its kind; a table, two chairs and an apple box, a sideboard, a gas cooker and a bed. It was indescribably filthy. The paper was hanging off the walls and ceiling and the woodwork had been varnished at the turn of the century. The tablecloth was a last year's edition of the Daily Mirror.

It reeked of stale sweat, cooked food, gas, filth and the contents of an over-flowing chamberpot.

Lying in the grubby bed was Jacky's moll. She was wide awake and not very pleased to see us. There was no sign of Jacky. Of more interest than Jacky's moll, however, was the classy fur coat hanging from a nail driven into the brown, varnished door. It was a beautiful coat of unmistakable quality. The young lady sat up in bed and never took her eyes off me as I examined the fur. I lifted it carefully from the nail and draped it over my arm. She shot out of bed and launched herself towards me. She wasn't a young lady at all. She was a vicious, filthy-tongued Glaswegian – a nasty piece of work. Spitting like a cat, she screamed: "Put it down you shittin' bastard, that's mine!"

Now, if when they embarked on their escapades, Jacky thought that he and his moll were similar to Bonnie and Clyde, then all I can say is that when she stood there in front of me, in her birthday suit, wrapped in a dirty army blanket, without her teeth in, she didn't remind me of Faye Dunnaway!

I asked her if the coat belonged to her or Jacky and she pretended not to know who Jacky was and went to put her teeth in.

"Bernard's in custody and Jacky's on the run. If you claim this coat is yours, then you will be taken into custody and have to do the explaining. If it's Jacky's, we'll leave the explanations to him."

After a lot of haranguing she was beaten.

"It's mine," she snarled, "but Jacky gave it to me."

As it was probably not Jacky's to give, I retained possession and searched the room, finding a fair quantity of goods which appeared to be the proceeds of crime.

We returned to Levenshulme and laid the property in front of Bernard who, when he was confronted with the loot, readily admitted to being involved with Jacky in committing 21 burglaries, but exonerated Sadie from all blame.

Later that night Jacky's luck ran out. Not trusting Bernard to escape capture and to remain silent, he decided to abandon his home, his girl friend and the stolen property and head towards London. Somewhat unwisely, he decided to leave the railway lines and head towards Knutsford where, in the dark, he positioned himself on the main road south and tried to thumb a lift from a passing police car!

Some four or five days previously, a night-watchman had been murdered in the area and intensive enquiries were being made to trace the killer. The Cheshire Police Officers, unable to take Jacky to London, were, nevertheless, in a position to give him a lift to the murder incident room, where he was asked certain questions concerning the death of the night-watchman. To establish his whereabouts at the time of the murder, Jacky confessed to committing a crime in Manchester and probably heaved a sigh of relief when he was handed over to the Manchester Police, who immediately charged him with the 21 burglaries Bernard had cited.

Amazingly, when Jacky arrived in Manchester, it was found that he had a wonderful sense of humour. He was a true comedian and fine mimic, with a line of patter far better than that of many music hall artistes. When he turned to crime, instead of the stage, he missed his true vocation. Keeping us well entertained whilst he did so, he made a full statement admitting to all his misdeeds. Without a doubt, he was a rogue and had been one all his life but, as a policeman, I must say it was a pleasure to do business with him.

The committal proceedings came and went with Jacky constantly bolstering Bernard's morale. He didn't seem capable of letting anything get him down and even refused to lose heart when Sadie visited him.

Prior to their sentencing at the Assizes, we visited Jacky and Bernard in the cells. Bernard knew that he was heading back to Borstal and had dropped his film star impersonations and, although inclined to be a bit sulky, he was doing his best to look nonchalant.

Also in the cell was a group of prisoners and Jacky was giving his final performance before bowing out from his audience. He had a string of gags, numerous impersonations and a cheery word for everyone. He comforted Bernard and then came to speak to us in a corner of the cell. He told us quietly that he knew he would be sent to prison and with his long record and a new conviction for 21 burglaries, it may even be for as long as five years. But hope springs eternal. Only two days before, one of Jacky's friends, with a similar record, had been sentenced at the same court to a period of two and a half years' imprisonment. Jacky was now hoping against hope for two and a half years, expecting three but fearing five.

It was mid-morning when Jacky and Bernard appeared before the judge and pleaded guilty. Through their counsel, as a plea for leniency, they both expressed regret for their actions and the suffering it had caused and broadcast their desire to turn over a new leaf. The judge seemed completely unimpressed and dealt with them separately and speedily. Bernard received a period of Borstal training. He looked at Jacky and gave him a slight nod before leaving the dock. Jacky stood to attention, facing the judge, his hands clenched firmly by his sides. He was accused of leading a useless life. But worse was to come; he blamed him for all Bernard's wrong doings. Here was a fully grown man, with a long criminal record, leading a 19-year-old astray. As the judge continued with his verbal lashing, Jacky's hands left his sides and he gripped the rail in front of him. A gasp came from the courtroom when the judge sentenced him to a term of ten years' imprisonment.

Jacky paled, his knees seemed to buckle, he swayed slightly and the hands gripping the rail were like parchment. But he recovered well, turned away and stumbled to the steps that led to the cells below. At the top of the steps he paused and looked around. He saw me. I was deeply shocked and felt very sorry for him for I didn't, in all honesty, believe that he deserved such a severe sentence – and he knew it. He tried to smile at me but couldn't, shrugged his shoulders, turned and walked down the wooden steps like a stricken clown.

□ □ □ □

The music coming from the Palais was too old-fashioned, the tempo too strict, the sounds too mellow, for it to be the normal Wednesday gig.

It was winter and one of those frosty nights when two pairs of gloves were called for. I entered the Palais out of habit more than anything else. It was if I had walked into a film set. I had stumbled into the area finals of the All British Ballroom Dancing Championship.

The women were all resplendent in exquisite gowns, the men, elegant in tails. They created a most marvellous scene as they floated gracefully across the floor. With style and rhythm, each sought to catch the judge's eye. It was spellbinding and I revelled in the enchanting atmosphere for as long as time would allow, then left the hall to make my way across the car park. Magical moments were not meant to last, for 17 Beat wasn't fairyland and there was work to be done.

Shortly after midnight I was on my way back to the section house by way of the Palais. During my absence, vandals had struck. Tyres had been punctured on each of the cars left in the car park and the area was full of men in evening dress, swearing and cursing, as they struggled with jacks and spare wheels. Grouped in the Palais doorway, sheltering from the icy wind, was a group of half a dozen ladies, shivering from the cold. With stoles and furs huddled around their bare shoulders, they waited patiently, with sequins flashing on their chiffon dresses and their gold and silver slippers glistening in the half light. Even though it was past midnight, they welcomed my approach, as Cinderella might have welcomed her fairy godmother and I rose to the occasion.

"Follow me, ladies."

I escorted them the 100 yards or so to the warmth of the section house, where old Paddy had never before experienced such an invasion. He stood to one side, a look of amazement on his homely Irish face, as I led the bevy of exquisitely-clad beauties past him. After a brief explanation, he became the perfect host, rushing into the parade room and turning the gas fire to its maximum setting, before beginning to look for seats for his guests

"Pull closer to the fire, dearie," – this to a tall, slim, blonde beauty, dressed in a mauve-coloured gown. He buttoned up his tunic to the neck whilst fussing round the sequined women like a broody hen. "Get on to the all night garages, Ninety-six," he instructed, "whilst I make a cup of tea for the ladies."

The night was turning from near disaster to pleasant adventure and, as Paddy dispensed the tea, he was delighted to find that he had many glamourous assistants. These rivals on the dance floor became all friends together, as the jovial Irishman treated each of them like royalty.

I returned to the car park and, with the arrival of a few mechanics, I organised the puncture platoon. As each car was made serviceable, I directed the driver to the station, so that he could pick up his partner.

In next to no time the crisis had passed and I returned to the section house where Paddy's Irish eyes were sparkling like two polished buttons. In his excitement, he used my first name over and over again, as he recalled each of the ladies.

"Did you see the one in mauve? Oh, and the tall, blonde girl in blue? And the dark girl in the red velvet cape? Jesus, Tony, I never thought the likes of that would ever happen to me!"

In years to come, the tale would become so embellished, that I expected to find both Ginger Rogers and Cyd Charisse included in the guest list!

Early Morning Call – 5 Beat

Stretching from Ardwick Green to the University and covering much of Chorlton-on-Medlock, 5 Beat was a slum, even by C Division standards. Its chief claim to fame was that David Lloyd George had been born there, in a modest two up, two down cottage. So, later on, he was well qualified in his desire to make Britain a country fit for heroes.

Prior to 1838, Chorlton-on-Medlock had been a township in its own right and many fine houses were built there by industrialists and wealthy merchants. Here they lived in style, whilst many of their workers were housed in cramped and unsatisfactory conditions, closer to the city centre. How times had changed. Most of the fine homes were now converted into common lodging houses, whilst nearby, the countless small dwellings were infested with vermin and had long fallen into disrepair.

As one might expect, in an area where people had to live with adversity, there were many unusual characters who, by their very presence, brought the dingy streets to life. For some of them, Brunswick Street Police Station was a focal point and all through the day they would call in, with either a story to tell, or a complaint to make. There were those who suffered from a persecution complex and heard whispers coming down the chimney, or sensed radar signals being diverted through the wall. One even suspected that coal gas was being piped through the water main, another, that the postman was an enemy agent who carried a transmitter in his bag. Then there was Mr Pepper who, each morning, received information on his Gobbles Magneto concerning planned Soviet aggression and came to the station in order that his daily bulletin, written in code on the back of a cigarette packet, be forwarded to Winston Churchill.

The first of the visitors would arrive, unseen, at 4.40 in the morning, Monday to Saturday, winter or summer. Heavy footsteps would be heard approaching along Brunswick Street, stopping when they arrived under the lighted front window of the station. After a slight pause and occasionally a small cough, the footsteps could be heard retreating down the street. Strangely, I never did venture out to discover who it was. We presumed that, whoever it was, had come to find out what time it was, as many people did, by staring through the window at the large round clock mounted on the office wall. Why he needed to look at the clock, it is difficult to say. He always came at 4.40 and he was so punctual that we could have set the clock by him.

The last of the regulars would arrive shortly before midnight, when a tall man, wearing a trilby hat and carrying a large, curved, meerschaum pipe in his right hand, would bounce into the station and rush along the corridor saying, "You know me, Sir, I've just got off that bus". He was known as Sherlock.

Here, at Brunswick Street Police Station, there was always something going on, with never a dull moment. On a winter's day, whilst the callers were arriving at the front office, the station coal would be disappearing out of the back. Over the dividing wall and into Nurse Duckworth's it would go by the bucketful.

"None of that ruddy slack, boys," she would call out from her side of the wall. "Let's have plenty of shiny nuts now." Or, if I was loading the coal from our side and giving her a load of 'old buck' at the same time, she would call, "Jesus, you're a rum sod you are, Tony. Saints be praised! But aren't you the one?"

This was accompanied by a loud raucous laugh and the sound of her shovel as she stacked the coal by her back door. As our 'chief medical officer' she was worth her weight in gold, as well as coal.

One of my favourite characters was a very deaf old lady who was known only as Trumpet. She was rather short and dumpy, had her hair crimped and set in a permanent wave and usually dressed in the style of the '20s with a large rope of amber beads hanging round her neck. She lived in one of the big houses nearby and would arrive late in the morning for a chat with the Station Officer. We always knew she was on her way, for we could plainly hear her heavy breathing as she slowly struggled down the corridor to finally lean on the office counter, smiling at everyone present, until she had recovered her breath. Not one to bother with those "piffling modern hearing aids", she carried an enormous bronze ear trumpet, on which there was a finely etched design. The only daughter of a family who had prospered in the textile trade, she had received a good, if somewhat genteel, education. She had remained unmarried and now, with the deterioration of the neighbourhood in which she had lived all her life and the death of her circle of friends, she missed stimulating conversation.

"The neighbourhood's gone to the dogs, no one with the brains they were born with, not a person worth speaking to since old Maud died and she was a moody old devil who was half round the twist."

So, it was an essential part of her morning, to arrive for an intellectual discussion with the Station Officers. Her favourite amongst the three regulars, was a rather rum old policeman called Jack Partington. When speaking to him, she would lean heavily, with both arms on top of the office counter and when she had finished talking, would raise herself onto her right elbow and place the trumpet to her ear, ready for the reply, whilst looking expectantly at Jack, with a smile on her lips. He would lean across the counter and shout into the blunt end of the instrument. I never tired of watching them conversing in this manner.

She enjoyed discussing the Arts, of which she knew a great deal and Jack, very little. But he never disappointed her because he was funny and made her laugh. On one occasion, he accused a well-known and highly-respected musical conductor of not knowing the difference between Offenbach's Barcarolle and Paganini's arsehole. She laughed so heartily that her elbow slipped off the counter and the ear trumpet was nearly brought to disaster.

Often Jack would be busy, particularly if he had circulations to write out. Then, with little time to spare, his patience would begin to wear thin and his choice of language would become even fruitier. This would please old Trumpet no end and she would give him a little smile and murmur,

"Now Mr Partington! Now, now! Let decorum be your bye-word at all times." She seemed to enjoy their conversations more on his busier days. "Very stimulating, Mr Partington, very stimulating," she would say, smiling broadly. "I'll call in again tomorrow morning to see how you are going on."

Leaning heavily on her walking stick, she would then turn and walk slowly out of the station with her ear trumpet tucked firmly under her right arm.

No matter which beat I was on, if I was on duty on a Saturday night, I would inevitably be thinking about where I would like to be, rather than where I was being paid to be. At midnight on a Saturday, most young men of my generation would be escorting a girl home from a dance, usually walking within sight and hearing of her friend, who was possibly accompanied by one of your friends. If this couldn't be arranged, then it was a case of walking the pair of them home and making conversation with both, whilst trying to work out how you were going to end up with the one you fancied.

It was shortly after midnight on a Saturday on 5 Beat and I was watching other young men escorting their girlfriends home and, of course, feeling quite envious of them. It had started to rain and I was doing the rounds of the domestics. I had, so far, attended four, all tame and short-lived affairs, ending abruptly at the sight of my uniform. Working in Chorlton-on-Medlock, I had anticipated that there would be more, for in those days, the duties of a Police Officer included the role of a social worker, especially when on night duty, before one o'clock on a Saturday or Sunday morning, when a constable patrolling such a densely-populated area, could be requested to attend as many as six or seven domestic disturbances.

In the majority of cases, the cause of the disturbance and the cure provided, were much the same. The husband, with only the prospect of working at a heavy manual job and spending his life in extremely poor living conditions, usually tried to ease the burden by getting blind drunk at the weekend. The considerate man would take his wife along to the pub and they would perhaps enjoy themselves. The man who chose not to, merely shelved his problems for a few hours, for when he arrived home, trouble would flare up, often resulting in him laying his hands on his good lady, sometimes quite heavily.

Usually, that was when the police were called, either by the aggrieved wife, or by a neighbour, anxious to get some sleep. Consequently, after half a dozen such calls in one night, the treatment almost became standardised. Bully the husband a little, threaten him with arrest, send him to bed and then quietly impress upon his wife the need for everyone, including herself, to keep the peace. In 90% of cases it worked – until the next time!

Occasionally, one met a hard case; the confirmed troublemaker and wife-beater who wouldn't respond to the usual advice. Then each case had to be treated on its merit and a different solution sought. Rarely was it possible to bring order according to the book, for no one can issue precise guidelines, or draw up a framework within which to operate, when dealing with such a variety of circumstances. Then it was a case of using one's initiative and, sometimes, the Ways and Means Act, to bring matters to a satisfactory conclusion.

I was throwing my cape around my shoulders and buttoning it against the wind and rain, when I saw the light flicker on top of the police box, which was only a few hundred yards away. My services were required. I entered the box, switched off the flashing light, opened my notebook on top of the desk and, with pencil at the ready, spoke to the operator.

"Ninety-six on Five Beat."

Her voice was pleasant.

"Good evening, Ninety-six. I've got a domestic for you, but speak to Sandy at Brunswick Street, he wants to tell you about it himself."

She transferred my call to Brunswick Street, where Sandy picked up the phone and gave me an address.

"I want you to go there. Skinner Harris is at it again."

"Skinner Harris?" It sounded like a character out of a Dickens novel. "Never heard of him, Sandy. Who's he, now he's at home?"

"No, you wouldn't have, you're too young. He only came out of prison last week after a five year stretch. One of his neighbours has come haring round to the nick in his nightshirt and slippers. Apparently Skinner's giving his wife the hiding of a lifetime and she's screaming the house down. Half the damn street's up in arms but, as usual, there's no one prepared to do owt about it."

This long deliverance was causing the asthmatic Sandy to wheeze into the telephone.

"Well, I've got his address, Sandy. I'm on my way."

Even though he was wheezing, Sandy was quick to interrupt me.

"Now just hang on, Ninety-six," he warned me, breathlessly. "Don't go rushing up there like a scalded cock. Skinner's a real bad bastard and I don't want you to go there on your own. A blue uniform's not going to frighten him, particularly if he's pissed. I spoke to Sixty-one a few minutes ago and he'll meet you at the corner of the street."

"OK, Sandy, I'm on my way," I answered, with a lift in my voice – the loneliness of the night was disappearing fast. Sandy detected the lift.

"Now watch him, Ninety-six," he cautioned, "he's a nasty swine and you won't meet many worse. You can bet your life he'll be expecting you. Oh, and by the way, don't waste any time at the front door. One of his party tricks is to empty the pisspot out of the bedroom window, so be warned!"

The chamber pot was a most useful item of sanitary ware in a division where most of the houses only possessed outside toilets and was kept under the bed and was considered invaluable in the home of a heavy beer drinker or an invalid. Sandy must have been really concerned, for it was the longest speech I had ever heard him make.

Sixty-one was on 4 Beat; six feet, one inch in height, well built, fair hair. Although he was twelve months older than me, I had served three months longer in the Force. We were becoming good friends and were on first name terms. His name was Harry.

I hurried to the other side of my beat and, as I approached the street where Skinner lived, could see Harry standing close to the corner, eagerly awaiting my arrival.

"Got the message?" he asked.

"Loud and clear."

"Know him?" asked Harry.

I shook my head.

"Never heard of him until five minutes ago. But old Sandy doesn't appear to hold him in high esteem."

"I don't know him either. Perhaps it's time we were all introduced."

No doubt he'd had the same warning from Sandy.

We walked down the short, dimly-lit street of small decrepit houses and noted that, in most of them, the lights were still burning in the downstairs rooms. But we didn't need to refer to our notebooks to identify Skinner's home, as the noise coming out of it was almost deafening. It wasn't an argument, it was a one-sided tirade of disgusting abuse. We walked towards the noise and, at the sound of our footsteps, several pairs of curtains twitched slightly. We were obviously expected. Then a door opened quietly and a man's head popped out.

"Psst, I'm the one who sent for you," he whispered hoarsely. "He's pissed out of his mind and bloody nasty with it."

Having said his piece, the head quickly popped back in and, just as quietly as it had opened, the door closed behind him. He had not had the benefit of elocution lessons but he certainly knew how to issue a warning.

We walked on tiptoe to the front of Skinner's home and I examined the door. It was secured with a Yale lock.

"Not much point in knocking," I whispered, "he probably won't be very pleased to see us. Sandy reckons he's pretty handy with the pisspot and

I've no intention of getting any wetter than I am already."

We walked to the rear of the house and entered a small yard where there were clear indications that Skinner had recently entered the scrap-metal business. Stacked near a dividing wall were several pieces of rusty scaffolding, four or five car wheels, a sump, several pieces of lead and, half leaning against the dustbin, an old cycle frame. Standing disconsolately beneath the kitchen window and half blocking the rear door, was an old clothes mangle. As we stood close to the mangle and listened, we could hear Skinner in the kitchen, cursing at the top of his voice and, within seconds, we discovered the main cause of his complaint – his supper hadn't been cooked to his liking; he preferred his fried eggs crisp. He was also giving voice to other complaints which, when put into plain English, implied that his wife was not very pretty, had been born illegitimate, that there had been other men in her life and that she didn't deserve him. Furthermore, if she dared to open her mouth just once more when he was speaking, he'd knock her bloody teeth out!

It wasn't an occasion for standing on formality, or reminding ourselves that an Englishman's home is his castle. We pushed past the mangle, I knocked on the door and lifted the catch and we both walked in.

Skinner had treated the kitchen as he had the backyard. The floor was littered with broken crockery and his supper of bacon and fried eggs. Standing near to the gas cooker was Mrs Harris, who turned away to hide her badly bruised and tear-stained face. She was making a second attempt to cook a supper to her husband's liking, by frying a pan of lamb's liver. She still had a good figure and had once been pretty, in fact, very pretty.

Sprawling on the kitchen table, still sporting his cap and muffler, a mug of tea in front of him, was the man we had come to see, the redoubtable Skinner Harris. He was big and swarthy with jet black hair and heavy jowls. What I first noticed about him, however, came as a relief. He was past 40, with a huge beer belly, which he was nursing in his big hands. No doubt he'd been a hard case, perhaps still was, but now he was past his best. I took them both in at a glance. Twenty years ago they must have made a handsome couple, but the years hadn't been kind, particularly to Skinner.

Skinner leapt to his feet. He was six feet two inches, burly and angry and didn't waste any charm on us.

"You Harris?" I asked in a neutral voice.

"I'm Skinner Harris. This is my house and out you bastards go," he bellowed, adding three f...s to make it sound convincing.

"Not until we've sorted out the trouble," I replied, calmly. "You're keeping half the neighbourhood out of their beds and we've had complaints."

Skinner had no intention of listening to reason and I thought that he was about to become violent.

"In that case, I'll soddin' well throw you out."

He directed most of his venom towards me, mainly because, being the slightly more experienced officer, I had opted to take the initiative. "Two baby-faced bastards in blue suits can't order me about," he screamed at the top of his voice, thrusting his face close to mine. "And, after I've sorted you two bastards out, the rest of the gets on this street will cop for it. Tomorrow there wont be a bleedin' window in sight."

His breath was as foul as the rest of him. Confusing ambition with ability, he gripped both Harry and myself by the upper arm and started to propel us towards the front door, steering us none too carefully past Mrs Harris, whose eyes never left the frying pan. His actions were rapidly putting us in a quandary. He must not assault us, he must not abuse his neighbours, or damage their property and neither must we be seen to lose face.

The first part of the journey from the kitchen to the front door was easy going and Skinner made good progress, but he should have realised that it was too easy, particularly when I opened the door for him. However, he was far too drunk to fully appreciate what was happening and only realised that the roles had been reversed when he found himself sitting on his backside in the middle of the street. He now had two alternatives – he could either run for it, or try and fight his way back into the house. He opted for the latter course of action and being drunk, aggressive and abusive in a public place, put him firmly in the drunk and disorderly bracket.

We arrested him and he was detained overnight, so allowing his neighbours to return to their slumbers. We were social workers without much finesse but with considerable adaptability. When sober, Harris was bailed, on his own recognisance, to appear at the Magistrates Court the following Monday morning. He appeared bright and early and brought his wife along to speak on his behalf. He entered a plea of not guilty and his wife, poor soul, gave evidence as to his recent good behaviour, informing the magistrates that he was now a reformed character, who was working hard to re-establish himself and that the outburst on Saturday night had been due to a misunderstanding on her part. She could understand, however, why the policemen had felt compelled to act as they did. It was quite a polished performance and it left me with the impression that it wasn't the first time she had been called upon to enact it.

At the end of the short trial, Skinner was convicted but, instead of the usual fine of 40 shillings, he was given a conditional discharge. Whilst still a conviction, it was a moral victory for him and we all knew it. To him a conditional discharge meant nothing. Worse was yet to come, for, as he left the courtroom, with his back to the magistrates, but in full view of the public gallery, he gave us the old, two fingered salute and, just in case we may not have fully understood, he mouthed, "Up yours!"

When I arrived for duty that night, Sandy was pushing his bike through the station door.

"How did he get on?" he asked, referring to Skinner's court appearance.

"He's got a conditional," I replied. "His wife turned up and told a cock and bull story. She made him sound like the Archbishop of Canterbury."

Sandy could see I was rather peeved.

"Well don't worry about it, son, he'll come again. People like Skinner always do. He couldn't keep out of trouble if he tried. And just think on, I've known his wife a long time, she's got to live with him, you haven't, so don't blame her entirely." I turned to move upstairs to the parade room when he called me back. "How did you find him on Saturday?"

"He's just a wife-beater and a loud-mouthed bully," I answered. "I can't imagine him assaulting many more policemen, Sandy. He's getting past it."

When I entered the parade room, Harry was telling those present about the morning's events.

"Stuck two fingers up at us, in front of every dead leg in the public gallery," he was saying vehemently.

The look on his face caused me to smile.

"Don't be so downcast, Harry. Just remember, he who laughs last, laughs longest."

"We'll never catch up with him again," said Harry, pessimistically. "He's too fly."

"Don't be too sure. There's more than one way of skinning a rabbit. The next time, we'll have to invoke the Ways and Means Act and see if we can skin Skinner," I laughed, with more confidence than I felt, but pleased with my play on words.

Five hours later, I was walking past Harris's home, when I remembered Harry's parting words.

"Put your thinking cap on and see what you can come up with."

Revenge on Skinner Harris was uppermost in his thoughts and it had become a very personal matter with him. It was cold and damp and the thought of Harris, warm and snug in his bed, didn't help. If he kept his nose clean for another couple of weeks, we would both have moved out of the area and, to all intents and purposes, that would be the end of the matter.

After a further 100 yards or so, I heard the sound of wires rattling against glass. A short silence, then a further violent rattling of wires. In the quiet of the morning, it sounded like a baby elephant shaking its rattle. Again a pause and then the sound of the rattle being shaken with renewed vigour.

"Testing for gas?" I called out humorously, knowing full well that the person responsible couldn't hear me, for he was as deaf as a post. Then I heard the voice I was expecting.

"Hud morning, nasty morning thith is, nasty morning."

I felt the wind blowing the rain against my face. It certainly was a nasty morning, a very nasty morning. The voice belonged to the knocker-up, who was on his early morning round and conveying the weather conditions to his clients. In my early days he was one of the policeman's nocturnal companions and, over the years, was reputed to have parted more northern couples than the Manchester Divorce Courts.

In Manchester, the original knocker-up had been the Watch, who had taken on the job during the industrial revolution. However, in 1839, when the Watch was disbanded and the Manchester City Police introduced, the duty and the perks were passed on, at the request of mill owners, to the first policemen. Unable to carry the regulation pole around with them, they used a child's peashooter and a pocketful of dried marrowfats with which to rattle the bedroom windows, as a supplement to a hefty knock on the door. This continued for a little while, until the Chief Constable of the day foresaw better things for his men and ordered the practice be discontinued.

In the 1890s, a retired Salford Police Inspector related how, in his early days, policemen used to wrangle fiercely over who should be allocated the lucrative working-class beats because, at threepence a week per household knocked, the take could be equal to a week's pay. When it was decreed that knocking-up was no longer to be a police function, inevitably, and much to the sorrow of those nineteenth century lawmen, privatisation took over and the job became a civilian one.

Eventually, whilst wandering about the streets in the early hours, a bond developed, between the knocker-up and the bobby, a fact which Lancashire author, Walter Greenwood, recognised in Love on the Dole. An early chapter opens with the Night Constable meeting Blind Riley who, armed with a 12 foot bamboo pole, with wires fixed to one end, trudged round his beat, usually from 3am onwards, knocking up bakers, railwaymen and millworkers, by the simple process of tapping on their bedroom windows with the pole and bunch of wires.

The knocker-up who covered the area in 5 Beat, lived in a little side street in Ardwick, no more than a few hundred yards away from the home of our wifebeater. He was old, had an equally old raincoat and flat cap, walked with a shuffling gait, was stone deaf and had a speech impediment. He would knock on the bedroom windows, wait until he saw movement behind the curtains and then, depending on the state of the weather, would shout, partly through his nose, "Hud morning, nice morning," or, "Hud morning, nasty morning". A creature of habit, he rose early, did the first part of his round and then went home at 3.40 for a bite to eat, resuming his duties at about four o'clock. When he went indoors for his breakfast, he would leave his pole leaning against the wall, close to the front door and it wasn't unknown for young and bored policemen to hide the pole in the back passageway, or even to attach a nut and bolt to the wires.

It was hearing the knocker-up, and knowing his modus operandi, that gave me an idea. I would arrange to have Skinner Harris disturbed from his boozy slumbers at a time which was quite alien to his nature. Whilst not the ultimate revenge, it would at least relieve some of the annoyance still felt after Skinner's insulting gesture.

I didn't immediately mention my idea to Harry, in order to gain time to perfect my plan. Should I slip a note through the knocker-up's letterbox enclosing two shillings and ask him to disturb Harris? Or should I do the job myself? I have a lisp, so the speech part was easy. I had imitated that shuffling gait several times and given a passable performance.

Between 3.40am and 4am, which was an ideal time, I had access to a first-class pole. Skinner lived no more than 400 yards from the knocker-up, so I would have plenty of time. By cutting out the middle man, it would also save me two shillings. I had decided – the job was mine.

When I met Harry, later that night, I outlined my plan to deprive Skinner of his beauty sleep and demonstrated my ability to imitate the knocker-up's speech and gait. He was suitably impressed. He not only liked the idea and gave me his blessing, but also offered his own contribution. His father, a retired policeman, rented a large allotment near Belle Vue and, like most allotment-holders, had a collection of flat caps and shabby raincoats.

"I'll have a cap and raincoat here for you by tomorrow night," he promised.

True to his word, when he arrived for duty the next night, he had a brown paper carrier bag which he placed alongside his refreshments in the cupboard and turned to give me a knowing wink.

"Picked 'em up at tea-time," he whispered.

After parading, we went into the enclosed rear yard and I tried on the coat. It was shabby and it was big, almost too big, for it reached down to my ankles.

"Perfect," said Harry, who was circling round me, not prepared to brook any argument. "Takes at least three inches off your height."

He handed me the cap and I chuckled in amazement. It was the biggest I had ever seen and ideal for the allotment holder who wanted to take home about five pounds of potatoes and a savoy cabbage for his Sunday lunch. I placed it on my head – it was the size of a manhole cover.

All that could be seen from a bedroom window would be the top of an enormous cloth cap, several yards of tatty raincoat and a long bamboo pole. We were in business!

At 3.40am on Wednesday morning, we watched from an entry, whilst the knocker-up shuffled down the street, leant his pole against the wall and entered his home. I doffed my helmet, handed it to Harry and put on the cap and raincoat.

"Right – off we go!"

I crossed the street, grabbed the bamboo pole and set off at speed towards Skinner's house, holding it out in front of me like a Bengal lancer in full attack, with a jovial Harry bringing up the rear.

We arrived at our destination unobserved and, raising the bamboo pole, I started to bombard Skinner's bedroom window with the wires.

"Rat-a-tat, rat-a-tat, rat-a-tat, rat-a-tat."

Within seconds l had got the hang of it and was soon beating a most marvellous tattoo on the window but Skinner was taking some rousing.

"Rat-a-tat, rat-a-tat, rat-a-tat, rat-a-tat."

It sounded as if someone was playing an old-fashioned set of bone clappers. I was determined that there would be only one winner in this early morning contest and that was going to be me.

"Rat-a-tat, rat-a-tat-tat."

Suddenly, the curtains were opened and Harris appeared at the bedroom window and could see what was happening. He didn't just shout his curses, that wasn't his style, he bellowed them out. His language was foul.

"What the hell's going on you stupid old ... ?"

Peering from under my cap, I shouted,

"Hud morning, nice morning thith is," and, shouldering the pole, shuffled slowly down the street.

Harris flung the window up to shout at my retreating back.

" ... hud morning ... off, you stupid ... !"

With a broad smile on my face and pretending not to hear, I continued on my way. Listening to him screaming was most rewarding and I knew that I couldn't have picked a better punishment for our victim.

At the back of his mind, Harris must have subscribed to the view that lightning never strikes twice, for the next morning it was even more difficult to waken him, although, to us, it was even more satisfying than Wednesday's morning call. Remembering the difficulty I had encountered with the heavy sleeper, I realised that there was no need for a gentle preliminary tapping, so let the window have a whole series of orchestrated blows with the wires. It sounded like a Spanish dancer who'd lost all sense of rhythm, whilst twirling round clicking her castanets. Skinner must have been drinking heavily the night before and it seemed that now I must first bring him back to life.

"Rat-a-tat-a-tat-a-tat-a-tat."

Without warning, the bedroom curtains were slashed back with an enraged bellow.

"Not you again, you stupid ... What the ... time do you call this? Quarter to four in the ... morning and a ... old pillock like you ... about with the windows. Now ... off!" he screamed.

"Hud morning, nasty morning thith is," I answered, imitating the knocker-up's nasal cry and made my way down the street, incorporating a double shuffle into my gait.

"That was perfect!" exclaimed Harry, "absolutely perfect! I can't wait for tomorrow."

"Tomorrow's the last time," I replied. "He's bound to be expecting me and, if he's true to form, he'll either have the pisspot ready, or come dashing out of the front door."

Harry took the spectator's view.

"What are you worried about?" he asked, eyeing the cap and raincoat. "There's enough waterproof gear there to withstand a force nine gale."

At one o'clock the next morning, I removed one of Skinner's options, by tightly connecting his front door knocker to his neighbour's. He couldn't come rushing through that!

At 3.40, dressed for the part and having borrowed the bamboo pole, we made our way to Skinner's. Whilst Harry remained hidden round the corner, I took up my position beneath his bedroom window. The old-fashioned sash had been raised by about nine inches and the curtains were drawn back in readiness. Skinner was indeed expecting the old knocker-up and it looked very much as if it was to be the pisspot treatment. Anticipating this, I had already decided on my tactic – tap and run – no point in heroics. Harry had suggested dislodging the pot, before the deluge, by trying to poke it out of Skinner's hands with the pole, but safety first was my motto. Cautiously I raised the pole.

"Rat-a-tat-tat-tat."

As anticipated, the window rocketed up and I heard Skinner scream out: "Cop for this you ... stupid old ..."

I could sprint the 100 yards in 11 seconds. Even without spikes, I must have made the first 20 in less than three, before resuming the shuffling gait. Behind me I heard a loud splosh.

"Hud morning," I called out, "nasty morning thith is, wain about."

Despite his years of slopping out in prison, Skinner had missed me by a mile. He was furious.

"I'll ... hud morning you, you ... old pillock, just you wait and see."

□ □ □ □

The public's image of a uniformed policeman varies. Some see him as a rather officious character, who struts about and delights in giving orders and issuing summonses. Others imagine him to be more human but assume that his job depends on his having to take a firm line to satisfy his senior officers. Many believe that quotas have to be met and a certain number of arrests made, before an officer qualifies for promotion. Not so. If such was the case, there would be precious few Chief Constables holding office today.

On C Division there were quite a number of constables who never went to court at all. A few of the older policemen, if sent there on an errand, would have had to ask directions. For years they had gone their own way, avoiding trouble and, indeed, avoiding work of any description. Putting pen to paper was something they could well do without and, to them, the word 'summons' might just as well have belonged to a foreign language. Certainly the thought of arresting someone and having to stand in a witness box and give evidence in a court of law, filled them with far more fear than it ever did the prisoner.

Sandy, our veteran Station Officer, was away on a well-earned vacation and such a man as I have just described was acting as his temp. It wasn't a job that this old bobby relished at all, stationed in a well-lit office, where any Tom, Dick, or Harry, could find him and possibly seek his advice.

During his time on the C, he had found better ways of spending his duty hours. He readily admitted that he wasn't any good at spelling and freely stated that there were men better qualified to handle the job but that, as usual, in this 'bloody outfit', no one was prepared to listen to him.

It was a warm evening and, to make matters worse, the gas fire was on at full heat. The old copper was sweating profusely and had tugged the collar of his tunic wide open, to reveal a neck like a rhinoceros. Standing at the tall desk in front of the open window, overlooking Brunswick Street, he was laboriously entering a number of circulations into the journal. He had grudgingly accepted them from the telephone operator and had left her in no doubt as to the humour he was in. I was standing at the counter immediately behind him, watching him continually wipe beads of sweat from his forehead with the back of a huge left hand, huffing and puffing like an overheated bull.

He turned and not too courteously asked me how to spell 'complexion'. I obliged and watched him return to his toils. He stopped, but this time with his back to me, barked out, "moustache?" I again obliged him. He continued to write, painfully slowly and then stopped and began to bite the end of his pen – stuck again! Obviously not having any confidence in my ability to spell this one, he dug into his tunic pocket and extracted a Gem dictionary, which he studiously consulted, before painstakingly resuming his writing. Curiosity got the better of me and I walked across the office and casually looked over his shoulder. I allowed myself a small smile of satisfaction when I saw that his much thumbed Gem dictionary had let him down. It seemed that the Derbyshire Police were seeking a young man in connection with the larceny of a motor car. He was 27 years of age, five foot nine inches tall, pale complexion, dark hair and moustache and dressed in a green jacket and blue overhauls!

Leaning idly against the counter, I watched him struggle; his nose no more than three inches from his pen and the tip of his tongue protruding from the corner of his mouth. Suddenly there was a rustling of paper and a whirring sound, followed by a large plop. The old copper jumped back in alarm, cursing loudly and knocking over a large stool as he did so. A parcel of greasy chips had come sailing through the open window, brushed against his face and landed messily on the journal. This outrage provoked an instantaneous reaction. He charged out to find the culprit with eyes blazing and mouth set like an equation sign. Outside in the street, nonchalantly leaning on the station window sill, was a drunken Irishman, who had apparently just disposed of his unwanted supper.

The old bobby was out of control. He grabbed the drunk by the scruff of his neck and the seat of his trousers, rushed him to the door and flung him into the station. The floor was highly polished and the Irishman slid on his backside along the 25 foot length of corridor, before ending up flat on his back in the kitchen, his arms and legs outstretched and a bewildered look on his face. The old copper stood over him, scarlet with rage.

Suddenly, as he began to realise the consequences of his actions, his fury subsided. For the first time in 20 years he had actually arrested someone. He swung round to face me, obviously seeking a way out.

"Charge him up, Ninety-six," he snapped, full of assumed authority.

"What with? Being drunk and throwing chips onto the station journal? You must be joking," I replied.

Having already found myself the fall guy for another old copper, I wasn't falling for this one.

"I insist!" His desperation showed in his eyes, which had taken on a pleading look. "It's, it's ... disorderly behaviour."

"Insist all you want," I countered, "as far as I'm concerned, if you want to call him 'Duncan Disorderly', he's all yours."

He stood there speechless for a few seconds, before springing into action. Again grabbing the drunk by the neck and trousers, he took two quick steps forward and, using an underarm bowling action, propelled him in the reverse direction down the corridor, until he ended up in a heap on the footpath outside.

We hurried into the office to watch through the window. The Irishman picked himself up, shook his head as if he'd been in a trance and staggered away towards Ardwick Green, without a backward glance.

The Wrong Trousers – 9 Beat

"Do you ever think about joining the DC?"

With less than two years' service, it was something I rarely, if ever, thought about, so I shrugged and replied:

"I don't suppose I'd turn the opportunity down, should I be asked, but I don't lose any sleep thinking about it."

Although what I had said was true, the answer rolled off my tongue, for I had been expecting the question for the last few minutes. I was talking to Cliff Gilmore, whose burning ambition was to be a detective and so the prospect of joining the CID was always uppermost in his mind. He thought like a detective, acted like a detective and, if such a thing is at all possible, looked like a detective. I say that because he was not too tall, thin in stature and had a pale complexion. He also walked with a rolling gait, a legacy of his Navy days. All things considered, he didn't exactly fit the popular image of a uniformed policeman. Cliff was born to be a detective and later, when a vacancy occurred in the CID and a less qualified man was chosen to fill the position, his disappointment was such that he resigned from the Force and left to start a new life in Australia. At a time when the city was crying out for good policemen, if ever there was a waste of talent, that was it.

But now it was shortly after 4pm, I was on 9 Beat, Cliff was on 10 Beat and we had just escorted the children over the school crossing points and were walking down Plymouth Grove, close to Manchester Royal Infirmary. Plymouth Grove had been a district of large superior Victorian houses but now many of them had been converted into flats or lodging houses and had become the haunt of pimps and prostitutes. After soliciting in the city centre, the girls would return with their clients and often consummated the deal, whilst staring up at an elegant stuccoed ceiling.

"There should be a vacancy coming up at Mill Street DO," confided Cliff, who was always in the know about such things, "I've put in an application. According to ..."

The conversation was halted by someone calling loudly, "Excuse me!" We looked around but couldn't see anyone. "Up here."

We allowed our gaze to travel upwards to where a man's head was poking through the attic window of a three-storeyed house.

"Do you want us?" shouted Cliff towards the heavens.

"Yes. Can you come up please?"

The man was attempting to shout in a hushed voice, as if not wishing to be heard by anyone else.

"Can't you come down?" we asked.

"I'm sorry, I can't. I've got problems," the man answered, again in a strangulated shout, which must have played havoc with his vocal chords.

So, we strolled into a small, overgrown and litter-strewn garden and entered the open door of a common lodging house. The hall floor was covered with badly warn linoleum, over which were scattered sheets of mud-stained newspaper. Oozing out of the kitchen and percolating throughout the house, was the smell of boiled cabbage. We made our way up the uncarpeted staircase, to where the man was concealing himself behind the attic door, whilst poking his head around the edge of it.

"In here," he croaked, and then withdrew his head quickly.

Once inside the attic, we soon saw his problem – he had no trousers. He was otherwise fully dressed in a navy-blue pinstriped jacket and waistcoat, white shirt and collar, silk club tie, blue socks and black patent leather shoes. It was the classic case, so often portrayed by Robertson Hare on the stage, but the first and only time I had encountered it in real life.

It was difficult not to smile. He was fiftyish, small, fair hair going grey, pink complexion and, if one allowed for the absent strides, a natty dresser. There was really no need to ask for an explanation, but Cliff couldn't resist.

"What happened?"

The man blushed and then trotted out a well-rehearsed story.

"I picked up a young lady in a bar in town, not suspecting for one moment she was a prostitute. Just someone to talk to. We had a drink or two, chatted away and then she invited me home to continue our discussion. We came back here and after talking for a few minutes, we made love. We were both a little tipsy and got fully undressed before we went to bed. Afterwards, she told me that she needed to use the bathroom and she dressed and went out. It was only when I suspected that she wasn't coming back, that I discovered my trousers were missing." He pointed to a white painted cane chair, as if it was partly to blame and, in a hurt voice, declared, "I put them over there."

He looked at us sheepishly, his story having run out. I cast my eyes round the sordid little love nest, whilst Cliff took out his notebook and got down to the nitty gritty.

"How much?" he asked in a flat voice.

"How much?" repeated the businessman, as though not understanding the question.

"Yes," persisted Cliff, "how much did you pay her?"

"Oh, er, two pounds," he stammered, somewhat abashed.

"Before?"

"Yes, before."

"Did you agree the price in town?"

"Yes," replied the businessman, squirming with embarrassment.

"And did she see you take the money out of your trouser pocket?"

The man nodded and again tried to blame the chair.

"Afraid so. There was sixty-five pounds in the hip pocket when I put them on that chair."

"Sixty-five pounds, eh?" muttered Cliff, "then I'll need your name and address."

At this, the man visibly panicked and his face turned crimson.

"I don't wish to make a complaint. I just want a pair of trousers."

"As soon as you told us that your trousers and money had been stolen you made a complaint," explained Cliff, in the same expressionless voice, whilst peering over the top of his notebook, with pencil poised.

"No, please, off the record," begged the man, as he nervously tried to thrust his left hand into a trouser pocket that wasn't there. "I'm a successful businessman and happily married with a grown up family." As Cliff still had his pencil poised, the man turned to appeal to me. "I'm not interested in the trousers, or the money. She can keep them. I just want a pair of trousers to get home in." He held his hands out, palms upwards in a desperate gesture. "No scandal, please. My eldest daughter gets married in three weeks' time and something like this could split the family."

"I need to know your name and address," persisted Cliff, "and the girl's description and the time and place you picked her up. You'll just have to trust us to be discreet."

The man looked at both of us in turn but, for some reason, he directed the question to me,

"There's no reason for my wife to find out about this, is there?"

I shook my head.

"None at all."

So he supplied Cliff with all the details, whilst I went to seek out the lodging house keeper. I located him where the cabbage smell was at its most pungent. He was of Polish nationality and, like many foreigners who find themselves in similar circumstances, he suddenly discovered that he had a language problem. Nevertheless, I took him upstairs and, as we entered the attic, the first thing he managed to say in English was:

"I dunno nuffin' about it."

I pointed to the Pole's trousers and then to the trouserless man. "Trousers," I said. When the Pole nodded, I raised my voice to a command. "Go and get him a pair."

He stood his ground. He understood alright, having come from a part of the world which respected authority, but he wasn't used to giving anything away. It was to be a battle of wills. Cliff, half smiling, looked across at us and awaited developments, confident that a scruffy, boarding house-cum-brothel keeper wasn't going to stand in the way of a quick solution. I caught hold of the Pole's shoulder and yelled into his ear, "Now!"

It seemed that I had overcome the language barrier, because he glared at the businessman and hurried downstairs, to reappear a few minutes later with a pair of evil-smelling trousers, that looked as though they had been worn throughout his years of journeying from wartime Poland. He handed them to me without speaking. Years earlier, they had possibly been cut out of a grey worsted material, but now they were so stiff with grease and dirt they could, quite easily, have stood up on their own. Only a brave or desperate man would touch them, let alone wear them, so I swiftly handed them to the complainant.

"Here you are, these will have to do," I said casually.

It was Hobson's choice. The businessman held on to the white painted chair and gingerly pushed first one foot and then the other into the vile article of clothing. Then came the moment of truth. With an involuntary shudder, he drew them up to his waist and started to fasten up the fly with the surviving buttons. He'd lost his pink complexion and had turned a nasty white colour, as if he was about to vomit. Whilst we stood admiring this act of courage, the landlord attempted to creep away unnoticed but Cliff only allowed him a yard or so, before stopping him in his tracks.

"Who's the girl who rented the room from you?" he asked.

The Pole shrugged his shoulders and pretended not to understand, but Cliff persisted until he muttered:

"Just a girl, Sir."

"She's called Veronica," said the businessman whilst trying to arrange his legs so that they avoided contact with the trousers. "She's about twenty, dark and good looking."

Trying to get the Pole to answer the simplest questions was like pulling teeth but he finally informed us that she lived close to Higher Temple Street, about half a mile a way.

Meanwhile, the businessman was keen to get away.

"I don't wish to make a complaint, Officer. She can keep the money."

We followed him out of the house and watched him walk away, Charlie Chaplin fashion, with stiff legs held wide apart.

"That'll dampen his ardour," said Cliff, then burst out laughing. "Christ, it looks as though he's crapped his trousers."

"If he has, I'm sure he won't have been the first," I answered.

Although the businessman hadn't wanted us to pursue the matter, Cliff had got the bit between his teeth and set off for Higher Temple Street, with me close behind. Arriving there a few minutes later, we began the search for Veronica. We walked from house to house, knocking on doors and asking the same questions, but to no avail.

"Veronica, did you say, about twenty? Good looking? Sorry, I don't know anyone of that description."

We appeared to be getting nowhere until, at eight o'clock, we knocked on a door which was opened by a fat, middle-aged lady.

"Veronica? No, never heard of her, but try Birdie Williams," she suggested, pointing to the house opposite, where the brown paint was flaking off the door in large strips. "He lives there and he knows most of the people round here."

We thanked her and crossed the narrow cobbled street. After a sharp knock, the door was opened by a young girl of about fourteen.

"Could we speak to Mr Williams, please?" enquired Cliff gently.

The girl looked back over her shoulder, whilst still holding the door open with one hand.

"Birdie," she called out, "two rozzers here to see you."

She was Mr Williams's daughter.

"Well? Show 'em in. Don't keep 'em waiting on the step, girl," answered a loud voice.

We walked along a narrow passageway and a man popped his head round the door frame.

"Come in, lads. What can I do you for?" he asked pleasantly, trying to be humorous.

On entering the room, we found there was an aviary where the kitchen should have been. Every wall was stacked from floor to ceiling with hundreds of bird boxes, occupied either by budgerigars, or canaries and on a table was a parakeet in a gilded cage.

"Mr Williams?" asked Cliff.

"That's me, Birdie Williams."

I looked across at him as he stood facing us, with his braces looped over a collarless shirt. There was something odd about his mannerisms but they seemed familiar. The small involuntary shake of the head, the sudden blinking of the eyes. Where had I seen them before?

"Freddie Williams, 'ave you heard of me?" he directed the question to me.

I chose the easy way out.

"You look familiar," I replied.

"Interested in the fight game?" he asked.

I now recognised the mannerisms for what they were; he'd had one fight too many. I looked at him more closely – between five foot six and five foot seven inches in height, no spare flesh on his bones, he must have fought at either welter or lightweight.

Cliff started to tell him the purpose of our visit but Birdie wasn't listening to him.

"Remember Jackie Brown?"

"Yes, everyone knew Jackie," I replied.

"Not Jackie Brown the Manchester flyweight. I mean Jackie Brown the Stockport boxer, fought at welter."

Of the hundreds of policemen on the Manchester Force, there probably weren't more than two or three who had known Jackie Brown, the Stockport fighter, but I was one of them. When I was eleven, he had ridden up on his cycle and broken up a fight between his half-brother and myself.

"I knew him quite well." I told him. "As a matter of fact, I knew all the family."

"Fought him at the Ardwick Blood Tub," announced Birdie.

"Had many fights, Freddie?"

"From when I was ten, until I was thirty. Fought as both amateur and pro. I've lost count of the number of bouts. The war finished my career." There was a spark in Birdie's eyes as he spoke about the fight game. "One of my best scraps was with Jackie Brown in 1939. Blood Tub was packed to overflowing. Caught him with a right in the third. Filled his legs full of whipped cream."

We stood back and watched him relive those three rounds, shadow boxing before a mixed audience of budgerigars, canaries and rozzers, with the parakeet hopping about its cage like a referee. As he delivered the final right cross, Cliff stepped forward.

"He mustn't have stood a chance," he murmured, trying to inveigle himself into Birdie's favour, before explaining the purpose of our visit.

When Cliff had finished talking, Birdie smiled at me and gave me a knowing wink as though, between us, we were now about to pull a fast one on him.

"Veronica, my arse!" he scoffed. "I'll tell you who that is, it's Vera Carmichael, Polly's daughter. Followed Polly on the game when she left school last year. Sixteen she is, never mind bloody twenty. Pinched his cash did she? Well she always was a cheeky little sod."

We both knew Polly well. The odds were that Birdie had sussed it out correctly. We bade our farewells and made our way to the front door.

"Remember me to Jackie Brown," said Birdie.

"Perhaps he won't wish to remember you," I joked, "especially the way that you treated him."

"Oh, he'll want to remember Freddie Williams OK, and if it's a budgie, or a canary you want, Birdie's your man."

We made our way to the home of Polly Carmichael, an overweight, brassy blonde with a loud mouth.

"We'll nip into the backyard first," said Cliff, "and have a scout round."

From the small enclosed yard, we could hear Polly's strident tones booming through the open scullery window. She was singing remarkably off key.

"There'll be blue birds over, the white cliffs of Dover, tomorrow just you wait and see."

It was the song of an extremely happy woman.

"She must have collected part of the tickle from Vera Veronica," smirked Cliff. Ever the budding detective, he went to the dustbin and lifted the lid. The smile on his face widened as he beckoned me to take a look. "We've hit the jackpot," he grinned.

Even he couldn't believe his luck. Lying on top of the ash and the trash, under a couple of overripe banana skins, was a pair of navy blue pin-striped trousers, a perfect match to the jacket and waistcoat we had seen that afternoon.

"There'll be love and laughter and peace ever after," Polly was bellowing in the scullery.

Cliff lifted the trousers from the bin and went through the pockets but found them empty.

"Come on," he murmured, "we'll give her something to sing about." Holding the trousers in front of him, he knocked loudly on the back door.

"The shepherd will tend his sheep," Polly sang, as she swung open the door with a flourish but the rest of the song froze on her lips and her mouth set in a straight line when she saw us. She gulped and looked quite sickly, as she caught sight of the pin-striped trousers suspended from Cliff's hands. "I know nowt about 'em," she screeched.

We pushed past her into the living-room, where a teenage girl, fitting the description of Veronica, had just got up from a chair and was heading for the front door.

"Hold on a minute," called Cliff. "Are you Vera?"

The girl nodded and looked at her mother for advice.

"She's done nothing neither," cried Polly.

"Call yourself Veronica?" asked Cliff.

"Sometimes I do," she agreed.

"Nowt wrong with that," complained Polly, "call yourself what you like."

"On the game, are you?" persisted Cliff.

The girl nodded but found herself in disagreement with her mother.

"No she's flamin' not," she snapped.

Cliff produced the trousers for the girl's closer inspection.

"We've got two witnesses who can positively identify you as the girl who stole these trousers and the sixty-five pounds which was in the back pocket? What have you got to say about that?"

"Bastard's had his money's worth," screamed Polly.

"No, he's not. Two pounds is the going rate, not sixty-seven," retorted Cliff, "and I'm speaking to Vera." He switched his attention back to the girl. "Now what have you got to say before I take you in and charge you?"

She looked shaken and again turned to her mother.

"Say nowt," advised Polly savagely.

Knowing that he didn't have a willing complainant, Cliff altered his tactics and handed Vera the trousers.

"Put the money back in the pocket and we'll see if we can square it with the man you stole them from." He looked sharply at Polly. "Sixty-five pounds now, or it's court for your daughter in the morning."

The game was up. Vera took forty-five pounds from a sideboard drawer, whilst Polly lifted her purse from the mantelpiece and took out the other twenty.

"She stole nowt! But if sixty-five pounds will stop her going to court, we'll pay."

The girl was either sharper than her mother, or else more trusting.

"I took the money by mistake," she confessed, "and he can have it back. I only took his trousers to teach him a lesson. I didn't know there was any

157

money in the pocket."

We cautioned a very despondent pair as to their future conduct and made our way back to Brunswick Street Station where, after explaining the situation to Sandy, we had the trousers and money booked in as found property.

The following afternoon, the businessman slipped into the station like a shadow, signed for his property and speedily left without uttering a word.

Although it is difficult not to agree that the pen is mightier than the sword, there are times, when keeping the peace, that the effect of the pen is not swift enough to defuse a desperate situation and other means have to be found. On C Division those occasions occurred only too frequently and a good man to have around was Reginald Hargreaves Hawley – Big Reg as he was called – a popular and highly-respected policeman.

Even in a Service where big strong men were common, Big Reg was exceptional at six foot three in his stockinged feet and made up of seventeen stone of muscle and sinew. Most of the time he was a genial Yorkshire giant; a big, friendly and unusual character who had a kind, if somewhat odd word, for everyone he met. Strictly teetotal and a non-smoker, he was also a keep fit enthusiast, who believed in a daily ration of press-ups, followed by a good dose of running on the spot, an activity which used to shake his terraced house on its foundations.

Generous and conscientious to a fault, he had become rather eccentric in his ways, keeping a 1921 Brough Superior motorcycle in the front room of his home. When patrolling his beat, he was far too conscientious to waste time crossing the road to stop and chat, as most of us did. When he caught sight of a colleague, he would maintain his stride and call out a greeting in a loud voice. In the first 12 months that I knew him, he would call out either, "Hello, young man. Test for gas," or, "Hello, young man. Come and see the ginger pussy". Test for gas was a reference to earlier war-time training and the ginger pussy was a large ginger tom cat, which habitually slept on the window sill of his home. During the following 12 months, he'd varied his greeting to, "Ho, ho, ho. Fat as butter, fed on custards".

I never got to the bottom of that greeting but it may have referred to an incident which occurred during my own Civil Defence training. A fanatical punter on the football pools, his form of greeting again changed during a severe winter, when the weather seriously affected the football league fixtures, causing many of the matches to be either abandoned or postponed. From that time on, until the date of his retirement, he would call out, "Hello, young man. 'A' for abandoned, 'P' for postponed".

When I first met him he was about 47 years of age and nearing the end of his service. He was always proffering me some advice.

"Keep yourself fit, kid. Deep breathing exercises, running on the spot, no supping or smoking, not too much of that there and if you ever feel off colour, then gargle with TCP."

Gargling with TCP was his remedy for all ailments. Six months before he was due to retire, he ruptured himself when he single-handedly lifted a motor vehicle, because someone lay trapped underneath it following a road accident.

He was neither a bully nor bad-tempered, but when the occasion warranted it, he was the most ferocious puncher; a bare fist fighter without equal. In his 30 years on the 'C', he probably didn't have recourse to use his fists, except on a few memorable occasions. I knew of five – four from hearsay and one which I witnessed.

His most celebrated fight had occurred 25 years earlier when, as a young probationary constable in the early 1920s, he had encountered a riotous situation outside the Drovers Arms on Ashton Old Road, Openshaw. At the sight of a solitary figure in a blue uniform approaching them, many of the rioters stopped fighting amongst themselves and joined forces to attack the giant young policeman. The big, powerful Yorkshireman, who few had ever heard of at this stage, stood his ground, fighting like a man possessed. He floored seven of his assailants so convincingly that they were still lying on the pavement when the prison van arrived, ten minutes later. An hour later and the licensee of the Drovers Arms arrived at Mill Street Station and placed a five pound note in the charity box, commenting to the Inspector on duty:

"I've seen many champion boxers in my time, but I've never seen anyone fight half as well as that young policeman and I don't suppose I ever will again."

Another time, after a drunken brawl on Ardwick Green, a Welsh rugby player picked himself up after Big Reg had knocked him down and came back for more.

"Hard case, he was," recalled Tommy Alker, "squat, ugly bugger. I've never seen anyone so fighting drunk. Just picked himself up off the deck and came boring in for more. Bloody hard to say who was the more surprised, the rugby player, when he realised that he'd been knocked straight back on his arse with one punch, or Big Reg, when the fellow picked himself up."

"How did it end, Sarge?" I asked.

Tommy Alker grinned as he remembered.

"Oh, Big Reg lost his temper a little and tanned him." He looked at me and then said, "I'm serious now, I honestly believe that Big Reg would have beaten Joe Louis in a bare fist fight."

It was in the aftermath of an Irish wedding celebration that I witnessed Reg's awesome punching power. He was then 48 years of age, still very fit, but obviously well past his prime. At about 11pm one Saturday night, I was standing in the office at Brunswick Street Station, listening to Sandy and another wonderful old policeman named Bert Goodwin, harking back to earlier and better days, when policemen were accepted as more influential members of society. Suddenly, with a screeching of brakes and tyres, a road patrol vehicle shuddered to a stop outside. Seconds later, the patrolman pounded down the corridor.

"Riot at the Blackstocks. Policeman in trouble," he panted.

It was well understood in the Force, that when road patrolmen received radio messages relating to trouble, they would invariably go in search of 'real' policemen, instead of racing to deal with the incident themselves, as they were equipped to do.

I grabbed my helmet and, with Bert close behind me, dashed out of the station to the waiting police car. Within seconds we were speeding away towards Upper Brook Street and the Blackstocks Hotel, a large brick built public house with a cobbled forecourt.

"Know anything about it?" asked Bert calmly.

"Not much," replied the radioman over his shoulder. "Irish wedding been going on all day at the Blackstocks. Suddenly the bloody pub erupts and a stupid waiter rushes outside and blows a bloody police whistle. A C Division lad hears it and, thinking another policeman's in trouble, runs to the scene and ends up in the midst of it. Apparently he's getting a right bloody pasting."

The lad on 9 Beat was Harry, my friend from the knockerup incident. "Get your foot down," I shouted at the driver.

In Upper Brook Street, the car was forced to stop some 40 yards short of the pub, by a large crowd of people, many of them bloodstained wedding guests, who were milling about and blocking the entire roadway and footpath. Bert and I jumped out of the patrol car and started to push our way to the centre of the action, passing a large group of Irish women who were acting in concert as they shoved, pulled and almost carried away, a big, blackhaired Irishman, who was cursing and struggling.

It was whilst passing this bunch of brawling femininity, that I noticed Big Reg. He was near the front door of the pub, towering in a protective fashion over Harry, who had been floored. Reg was on 10 Beat and had reached the scene only seconds before. He was standing erect, left shoulder slightly dipped, enormous fists, like full hams, held in the old-fashioned pugilistic manner and his huge frame planted in a pair of boots the size of coal barges. I glanced at his face. The gentle expression had vanished. Even from a distance he looked angry, very angry.

Warily circling him, in an aggressive manner, were three powerful Irishmen, all in their early or mid-20s, each of them more than six feet tall and fighting drunk. The tallest, a man of about 26, advanced on Reg menacingly. Reg, standing on the balls of his feet, swayed slightly, then hit the man with his left hand, causing him to keel over sideways in a crumpled heap on the footpath. The second Irishman rushed in but, before he could land a blow, Reg pounded two lefts to the side of his head in rapid succession and, without more ado, the man dropped to the ground as if he had been pole-axed. Then Reg advanced on the third man and dropped him with a thunderous right hand to the head. Four mighty punches, which had sent three big men sprawling, immediately quelled

160

the affray. None of the other guests seemed to want to suffer the same treatment and they dispersed noisily, but without further persuasion. I went over to where Harry was staggering to his feet.

"OK?" I asked.

He nodded, then caught sight of the man that the group of women were leading away.

"That bastard's as bad as any of them," he called out. "Him and these three gets were at the centre of it all."

Bert and I went after them. The man being led away by 20 or so women, of all ages and sizes, was the bridegroom. Apparently, it was considered that, at this time of night, he had other, more important, duties to perform. Well to the forefront was the bride, accompanied by a tall, dark bridesmaid who, curiously, was still carrying a posy in her left hand. I have rarely heard such foul language as was emanating from that covey of drunken beauties. We pushed our way into the midst and caught hold of the bridegroom.

"He's just assaulted a policeman and he's under arrest," Bert shouted.

As we turned away with the groom, it was as if a fox had just stalked into a hen-house and caught hold of the cock. In a flash, all hell broke loose. Blows from fists, handbags, umbrellas and shoes were rained down on us. A young woman attempted to scratch my face and kick me in the groin, whilst one old crone even hit out at Bert with her walking stick.

"Bastards, bastards, English bastards," they squawked.

There was no let up in the intensity of their assault until Bert came to the rescue.

"Can you manage him on your own, Ninety-six?"

"Think so, Bert," I nodded, breathlessly.

He let go of the groom and set about the pack of women with the flat of his hand, swatting them like a swarm of flies. Harry rushed up to join us and grabbed the bridegroom's other arm. With Bert guarding our backs, we hustled him away to the nearby police box, where Big Reg and the two road patrolmen had taken the other three prisoners.

When the prison van arrived, they were taken to Mill Street and charged, not with causing an affray, as they should have been, but with the good old standby; drunk and disorderly. All four were steelworkers from Sheffield and when they were asked if they wished to reply to the charge, the tallest and most marked, spoke for them all:

"We'll never come to Manchester again, Sir."

It wasn't said spitefully, but truthfully and with sorrow.

The following Monday morning, prior to attending the Magistrates Court, it was necessary to attend Court Parade at Mill Street Station where, in the Superintendent's office, we had to explain the circumstances leading to the arrests. The Superintendent, who had been briefed by the Charge Office Inspector, listened carefully as Big Reg supplied the barest details of the incident.

"Hm, after Sixty-one had been assaulted, what happened then, One two five?" he asked. "What precisely happened once you'd arrived at the Blackstocks?"

I had seen what had happened. Reg had saved his colleague from possible serious injury and had stopped a most serious affray. I don't know of any other person who, single-handedly, could have done that. I waited for the big man's reply, which was a model of understatement; worded with old-fashioned simplicity and characteristic of only one policeman – Reginald Hargreaves Hawley.

"Sir, when I got there I saw three men attacking Constable Sixty-one. I immediately went to his assistance and engaged them in fisticuffs."

Twenty years after Reg's retirement, a friend of mine called to see him. Apparently he was in the scullery, dressed in slacks and singlet, running on the spot and still talking about the healing qualities of TCP. He was 70 years of age.

At the Sharp End – 29 Beat

The mere mention of 29 Beat brings back memories of two different, but related subjects; civil defence and first aid. Situated in the centre of the beat was Mill Street Station and it was there that we were trained in these disciplines. I cannot pretend to remember the things I learnt, only that167 it was very little, but I will never forget how relaxing it was to be away from the daily grind and particularly the fun we young constables infused into the courses.

After the Second World War, both central and local government planning, in terms of civil defence, had been greatly influenced by the arrival of the atom bomb. Newsreels of the bombing of Hiroshima and Nagasaki, shown to an almost unbelieving public, had shocked even a war-hardened nation. Devastation on this scale had never been seen. That it had been caused by a single bomb, was not only frightening, but gave cause for grave concern. Should such a disaster befall a city in Great Britain, then we had to be prepared. Large areas would have to be evacuated and the police be in a state of readiness, with the expertise to deal with any emergency.

In Manchester we were ready. In compliance with Section One of the Civil Defence Act, 1948, the city police had established a War Duties Department. Consequently, it was arranged that every member of the Force should receive a period of training which could be updated whenever any new and perhaps even more horrific weapons were invented. Human nature being what it is, war training in times of peace was taken less seriously that it should have been, both by the young and old alike and, I suspect, even by one or two of the instructors.

One Inspector, angry at having to release men from operational duties to attend a course, remarked:

"Bloody atom bombs! Who the hell would want to drop one on the 'C'? And even if they did, who'd ever notice?"

In many respects, I had to agree with him and history proved him to be correct when he went on to say:

"Waste of bloody time and money. Jobs for the boys," referring to the instructors who were struck off from normal police duties to occupy what he called a 'bloody cushy billet'.

In the early days, the War Duties Department consisted of two Sergeants, who specialised in stirrup-pump drill, firefighting and rescuing people from bomb-damaged and burning buildings. Waste materials would be ignited in a small wooden hut and they would then demonstrate how to tackle the blaze with a stirrup-pump. Then it would be our turn. One constable would pump like fury, whilst the other would slide into the hut on his stomach and direct the jet of water onto the fire. A Sergeant would push his head through the window space to give instructions and accidentally receive a jet of water in his face. This was considered good fun and par for the course.

After the blaze had been extinguished, someone would call out, "Knock off and make up," and that would be the end of the stirrup pump drill! What was so incongruous was that both firefighting Sergeants were immaculately turned out – their smartly-pressed trousers had razorsharp creases and they affected upper crust accents, similar to the Western Brothers. Not quite what you would expect of front-line troops but much more in keeping with 'headquarter wallahs'. Both were ambitious men who, after a short period of time, were transferred to duties more in keeping with their appearance.

The next instructor to arrive on the scene was Horace Lloyd Perkins, an Inspector, who seemed determined to take his cushy number seriously. Once he had settled in, he proved to be a mixture of enthusiasm and gullibility; a big amiable overgrown schoolboy, who saw the cold war in the same way as most people had received the invasion threat shortly after the miracle of Dunkirk. In selecting him for the position, it was as if the Chief Constable no longer took the nuclear threat seriously but, instead, was concentrating his attentions on the more immediate problem of combating crime.

Horace entered into the spirit of his new post, as he did most things; wholeheartedly and with a determination to succeed which few could rival; tackling the job as if our lives depended on it. He quickly established new routes of evacuation from the city, preferring long, straight, wide roads leading south. He indented further supplies of steel helmets and rubber wellington boots and obtained a Geiger counter and a radioactive isotope. Then he introduced us to the control room, which was fast becoming his pride and joy and seemed to be cast on the same lines as the one operating at Biggin Hill during the Battle of Britain. His unrestrained enthusiasm for entering into areas where other policemen feared to tread, naturally left him exposed to his fair share of mickey-taking but, Horace being Horace, it was all very gently done and rolled off him like water off the proverbial duck's back.

One Tuesday, I walked into the parade room at Mill Street Station and, after nudging my way between two young burly figures, I leant against the tall desk. I was on afternoons and idly watching Harry as he studied the daily duty sheet (DDS). It was necessary for everyone to read it carefully, as it may have contained variations to their planned duties and woe betide anyone who missed an alteration concerning them personally.

Harry looked across at me.

"Who's the lucky one then? Which blue-eyed boy's been awarded two early turns on Thursday and Friday?" He flipped the clipboard, which held the DDS, across to me saying, "Civil defence training – why should England tremble?"

I examined the sheet and saw that I had been earmarked for day duty (9am – 5pm) on Thursday and Friday of that week and joyfully rubbed my hands together in front of the others. My expression of glee had nothing to do with the course itself - it was the prospect of the two evenings off duty later in the week.

On the Thursday morning I ran up the stairs at Mill Street and tried to enter the lecture room, only to find my path blocked by a mountain of white dustsheets and paint-splattered planks. I eased the door ajar and pushed my face round the edge of it. Kneeling behind it was a man in white overalls, with one arm, almost up to his elbow, in a large drum of emulsion paint which he stirred round and round with a brush handle.

"You're being decorated," he called out when he spotted me. "Your lot are in the bike shed, mate, wherever the 'ell that is."

So I crossed the cobbles of the rear yard to the cycle shed, a large wooden structure which had been built as an ARP post in the war years and which, if used exclusively as a cycle shed, would have been big enough to accommodate every machine entered in the Round Britain Milk Race.

Horace was standing just inside the door, none too pleased with the move but undaunted and determined to make the best of things. He was addressing a group of constables who were gathered round him.

"Now this is what it could be like in wartime. We'd be expected to improvise from day one and this could be the ideal training for the real thing."

There were 16 policemen allocated to the course, four from each division. I was one of three young constables selected to represent the 'C', the fourth officer being Inspector Cartwright, a long-serving taciturn Scot who, because he was rarely seen to smile, had been nicknamed Ned Sparks, after the poker-faced American film star. I later got to know Ned well. He was stern, just, scrupulously fair in all his dealings and represented the finest type of policeman. He had a wonderful sense of humour but, in order to maintain some semblance of discipline on the 'C', he kept it well and truly hidden behind his expressionless mask.

The course duly got under way and the rest of that morning Horace spent updating us in our firefighting techniques. A veteran of the Manchester blitz, Ned stood quietly to one side, taking an interest in the proceedings, without actively joining in. No doubt he had been doused with water on previous occasions and didn't relish a repeat performance. He was the same rank as Horace, but a far more experienced and capable policeman. He even allowed himself the luxury of a smile as he watched Horace, dressed in his outfit of blue overalls, wellingtons and steel helmet, chasing three young firefighters round the yard with the Geiger counter held at the ready, as he sought to establish whether we had been contaminated by radiation.

All in all, it had been a most active and enjoyable morning and we had worked up a good appetite for lunch. Lunch at Mill Street was invariably something with chips. The cook's name was Gladys and it was the only way she cooked potatoes, justifying this by claiming that, "the lads love my chips," and she was certainly an expert chip-maker.

The first afternoon of every civil defence course was always devoted to the showing of films and the content never varied. Having seen the bombing of Hiroshima and Nagasaki once, there wasn't an awful lot to be gained from viewing it all over again. Horace blacked out the cycle shed and set the projector in motion. Soon, the constant flickering of the screen, the commentator's monotonous tone and the effects of Gladys's steak and kidney pie and chips, began to take their toll. One by one, we gradually nodded off, some dozing fitfully, others falling into a deep sleep; so deep, in fact, that even the exploding of two atom bombs didn't disturb them.

The following morning, we were introduced to the mysteries of the Geiger counter. In a heavy, lead-lined box was a piece of radioactive material which certainly set the Geiger counter buzzing. After a lecture as to its use, it was time for war games. Hide and seek, the teacher had called it, when I was in kindergarten. It involved Horace hiding the box for us to find by the skilful use of the Geiger counter. Firstly, however, he showed us how it should be done. Whilst he remained in the cycle shed, one of us hid the box. At a given signal, he would lead the rest to find it. He didn't set the limits of the search area, but assumed that the dangerous, radioactive element would be hidden within the confines of the police station.

The hunt got under way and, after a full hour's search, with Ned and a number of young constables walking behind him, like a party of tourists, he was anxiously poking the Geiger counter into every dark recess in the station, aware that he was fast losing face. Added to that, he was becoming increasingly agitated at the thought of someone having lost the dangerous isotope, for which he was personally responsible. Finally, he had to admit defeat, only to be told that two of the lads had got it hidden, but under guard, behind the nearby tripe works.

Then it was time for lunch and lunch on Friday was always the same – fish and chips. Over his midday meal, Horace speedily put the disappointment of the morning behind him, particularly when he found himself sitting at the same table as two attractive lady telephonists. In such charming company, he put all thoughts of the wasted morning and the nuclear threat to one side and set about making their day memorable.

"Siberia, that's where Stalin will send us if he's allowed to gain control. He'll treat the Armed Forces and the Police alike." He looked authoritatively at the two girls over a forkfull of battered cod and mushy peas. "Yes, both you and I, Siberia – that's where we'll end up, make no mistake about it, Siberia."

By the afternoon he was again ready to set about the task of preparing us for the holocaust. But, this time, we knew that the battle was to be fought at a higher level. He had doffed his overalls and gumboots and now wore his best day uniform; the tunic, complete with his good conduct medal ribbon over the breast pocket, his polished steel helmet worn with the chin-strap down but angled in a jaunty defiant fashion. He had cut short his refreshment period and had converted the cycle shed into an auxiliary control room, by pinning enlarged photographs of the bombing of Hiroshima and Nagasaki on the far wall and placing a double desk in a prominent position in front of them, as if to impress upon us that we were entering the nerve centre. On top of the desk, he had placed a large card on which was printed, CONTROL ROOM.

Horace was, of course, in charge and he sat in the centre of the desk looking at us seriously from under the rim of his steel helmet, doing his best to look like Jack Hawkins. In deference to Ned's seniority, he had felt obliged to appoint him Joint Controller, a position which Ned accepted with a semblance of a smile, as he took his seat by Horace's right side, before once again donning the poker-faced expression.

Horace then presented us with a scenario and it was, indeed, bad news. We had entered a state of war. An atomic bomb had exploded over Manchester and it was necessary for us to evacuate the city along the predetermined routes. Horace, and this is important for the story, had set up the main command post in an imaginary bakery which had escaped damage. He must have regularly established himself in a bakery, for next to the control room sign, he placed another, which read, COMMAND POST and then, in case anyone should confuse this with a lesser command post, he placed another sign next to it which read, BAKEHOUSE.

He was to bring order to the city and control the evacuation, whilst we were to be his outposts at the sharp end of the action. I now saw how busy he'd really been at lunchtime. In each corner of the cycle shed, he had positioned a small square table which had been assigned a card reading either A, B, C, or D. Teams representing the territorial divisions were now sent to their respective outposts, with instructions to update Horace as to the extent of the damage inflicted in their area and to list any requirements needed to deal with the situation. Horace was to maintain a log, which he did in copperplate handwriting. As all communications were supposed to have broken down, messages had to be handwritten and sent via a runner.

After a few minutes spent discussing the situation, Horace requested that we make our assessments and then dispatched his runner, an elderly asthmatic constable, to collect them. He was to take our assessments back to Ned who, having digested the contents, together with a carefully-studied list of our requirements, then relayed the information to Horace, for entry into the log.

A division's report was called for first and didn't provide Ned with good reading – heavy damage in the city centre and many office blocks ablaze – number of casualties unknown, but expected to be heavy. Horace diligently made the appropriate entry into the log, before turning to his joint controlee, with pen poised:

"Requirements please, Mr Cartwright."

Ned again consulted the message before supplying the information that Horace was seeking:

"Firefighting equipment, medical aid, Geiger counter and transport."

B Division's report was even worse – citing widespread damage, thousands of casualties, the cessation of all orderly life and requesting medical aid, firefighting equipment, police reinforcements and transport. Horace looked up from entering the log;

"A very serious situation, Mr Cartwright," he pronounced, loud enough for all to hear.

Ned looked across at the darkened corner where, in the C Division outpost, three young constables sat without any supervision.

"Yes, very serious indeed, Horace," he replied, "very serious indeed."

Then it was our turn. The runner handed our assessment to Ned and we each studied his face as he read it. There was a twinkling of the eyes and the ghost of a smile playing across his lips, as he digested the latest information. He then began to read slowly and with great authority:

"C Division to Command Post at Bakery. Reporting total destruction. The entire population destroyed."

"Total destruction, eh?, that's bad," murmured Horace, as he bent to record it in the log, "even worse than the B."

He looked up when he had finished and paused to adjust his helmet, which had fallen over his eyes whilst writing.

"Requirements please, Mr Cartwright?" he called out.

Ned purposely let his eyes stray to the bakehouse sign.

"One small brown and three large custards, please."

How many times Ned was later to tell that tale I don't know, but right up to the date of his retirement he would ask me if I still enjoyed a custard tart.

□ □ □ □

A policeman was expected to be a man of many parts; not only did he have to have a good working knowledge of the law and be well versed in civil defence duties, but he was also required to hold a current first-aid certificate.

The authorities attached great importance to the latter but, because of the close proximity of such good hospitals in Manchester, a fine Ambulance Service and the 999 telephone system for emergencies, I regret to say that most young constables attached less importance to the subject than they may have done in different circumstances. It was treated as something of a joke and on a division with a reputation for heavy drinking, the prescribed medication in answer to many a medical question was to give, 'copious draughts of fluid to the patient'.

If, when talking shop, a policeman informed another that first-aid was rendered, he would mean that someone, usually a violent prisoner, had been given a good hiding.

To obtain the required first-aid certificate, one had to pass an examination set by Dr Blench, the police surgeon. Old Blench was a very odd character. Prior to the National Health Service, part of his duties entailed visiting and prescribing medication for sick policemen and, to many of them who kept a packet of cigarettes ready for him on the bedside cabinet, he was known as a sympathetic friend. Now that this position had been denied him, much of his day and night seemed to be spent examining drunken drivers, visiting the Coroner's Court, or performing postmortem examinations at the small mortuaries which were attached to police stations.

Working in an area with a high sudden death rate, the PMs became his speciality and frequently, on a January or February morning, he would be expected to perform up to eight of them, usually treating the police reserve man to half-a-crown and expecting him to stitch up afterwards. Not a big chap, he smoked like a factory chimney. But, as if in warning to a young policeman who stood beside him whilst performing a PM, he would show how nicotine affected the lungs and all this whilst puffing away at a John Player's himself.

To attain the required first-aid standards, a course of instruction was necessary; 12 two-hourly lessons on Wednesday afternoons at Mill Street Station, 2.30pm – 4.30pm, which gave the constables on the morning, afternoon and night reliefs, the opportunity to attend. The instruction was given by Jack Dovey, a 22-stone, pot-bellied, beat cycle repairman. Now coming to the end of his service, the corpulent Jack had been giving first-aid instruction for many years, and it surprised no one who knew the system, that both the beat cycle repairman, and all of his pupils, enjoyed a 100% pass rate.

To compensate for attending lessons in their own time, young constables were not paid overtime, but received three hours 'time due'. The time due system was a great boost to their social life, because three hours time due would allow a man to parade at 2pm on the afternoon shift and retire from duty at 7pm. Thus shiftwork was made much more bearable. Confident in the knowledge that no one had ever failed to pass the examinations, more attention was given to securing three hours time due and the pleasures it could bring, than to gaining vital medical knowledge.

For 12 weeks, each Wednesday afternoon, the large lecture room echoed to the sound of 14 first-aiders, practising their new found skills. Bandages, slings and tourniquets were applied with varying degrees of skill. Various methods of resuscitation were practised, often with quite unnecessary zeal, bordering on violence, when sufficient pressure was applied to damage a friend's lungs. We all had to recite Pretty Little Suzy (pain, loss of power, shock), a hundred or so times. Jack had a coloured chart, which he used to explain the circulation of the blood. Milk was prescribed to counter the effects of certain poisons and warm, weak tea given to those in shock.

At the beginning of the course, St Johns Ambulance books were handed out for us to take home and study at our leisure. Published five years earlier, they appeared to have never been opened and had been returned by previous students in the same pristine condition as when they had left the printing press.

Then came the examination and for us the fun was over. By this time, Dr Blench was getting old and grumpy and, to make matters worse, during the night prior to our first-aid examination, he had been turned out of his bed twice to examine drunken drivers. This was well before the days of the breathalyser and a police surgeon had to examine each and every one of them.

Some 14 constables sat the examination. After bandages, slings and tourniquets had been inspected and torn apart in disgust, each man was examined separately by the tetchy doctor in a small ante-room, the rest of us patiently waiting outside. Bertram, the world's worst first-aider, was first through the door. It was he who set the standard – if he passed, we all passed. After a few minutes, we heard raised voices. Old Blench was certainly losing his temper. After about ten minutes, some five or six minutes longer than had been anticipated, Bertram re-appeared, looking rather dejected. He gave the thumbs down sign and said, "dipped".

It was most unexpected and the first time that such a thing had happened, but we weren't too shocked. When it came to first-aid, Bertram was, as I said, the world's worst. The next candidate went in – raised voices – exit – thumbs down – dipped. Now this could be serious, for this lad was as good as the rest of us. We could be facing a catastrophe.

St John's Ambulance books were rapidly produced and distributed by Jack Dovey and, in the next 15 minutes, during which time, apart from Blench's raised voice, you could hear a pin drop, I did more work than I had during the entire course. When my turn came, I was relying almost entirely on the circulation of the blood and Pretty Little Suzy. Blench was red in the face and bleary eyed. I sat before him and resorted to smiling pleasantly and trying to look confident. It got me nowhere, for he immediately demolished my composure by asking questions about poisons and their effects, which even Lucretia Borgia and her family would have struggled to answer.

Needless to say, I failed. I found myself in good company, for only two of our number actually passed. When the results arrived on the Superintendent's desk, it took him the best part of the morning to get over the shock but, once he had, he was livid. He sent for the 13 failures – for he included Jack Dovey in that category – and in a thunderous voice imparted some good and some bad news. The good news, from our point of view, was that he unfairly blamed Jack Dovey for the disaster. Better still, he ordered the 12 young ones to undertake another 12 week course of instruction – great for our social life and it helped to pass the winter on nicely.

The bad news was that he not only put Jack Dovey's instructor's job on the line, but also his cushy cycle repair job as well and threatened to put him back on the beat. It would have been nice to report that we, seeing the unfairness of it all, felt rather sad for old Jack. But not a bit of it, we simply rejoiced at our own good fortune.

A further 12 week course of study prepared 11 of us for the examination and, without a doubt, we had achieved the required standard. Twelve years at Guys Hospital wouldn't have prepared Bertram, and Jack Dovey, realising this, offered him the same rights that a prisoner is allowed on an identification parade.

"Do you want to choose your position, Bertram?" he asked.

Bertram made his point by replying,

"I'm buggered if I'm going in first. I'll go in last."

The doctor was a friend of the first-aid instructor and knowing that the sword of Damocles hung very obviously over his head, he now regretted his previous tetchy behaviour and was determined not to allow us young upstarts to affect Jack's career. He'd obviously been warned about Bertram's weaknesses, for he allowed his eyes to feast on his divisional number before the examination began and even gave him a reassuring smile.

First there was the obligatory bandaging session, which he merely examined visually, with no tugging or pulling of the knots and, in Bertram's case, from a distance of six feet and only glancingly at that. He wasn't taking any chances. Afterwards, there was no separate examination. He sat at a table, one empty chair facing him and the 12 entrants seated in two lines behind the empty chair. Dr Blench was kindness itself.

He called us forward by divisional number. In turn, we each sat on the chair facing him as he asked the simplest of questions – one each – and the first 11 answered correctly. Now it was Bertram's turn. The normal sound level had dropped to a deathly hush.

"If your patient has fallen off a high ladder, how would you know if he had broken his back?"

There was a long silence, then a whisper, indeed a chorus of whispers from those sitting behind. None of the whispers seemed to reach Bertram, who sat as silent as a tomb. He not only had a mental block but seemed to have frozen as well. The question was repeated by the doctor, who now resorted to putting leading questions. But Bertram's lips refused to move. Dovey was in despair. However, all was not lost, Blench rose to the occasion. He left his chair and stood patiently behind Bertram, waiting for his answer and, when none came, jabbed a needle into his backside.

"Did you feel that?"

"Yes," came Bertram's swift reply, as he vigorously rubbed the injured part.

"Now, think carefully before you answer. Would you have felt it if you had got a broken back?"

This broke the spell and Bertram's lips finally moved. He may have said, "no"; everyone else certainly did!

The doctor returned to his chair and proceeded to mark the papers. He looked up at Dovey.

"Much better this time, Mr Dovey. I'm pleased to say that they have all passed."

There's room in the Police Service for all. Bertram, who was an excellent penman, later became a Coroner's Officer, where his lack of first-aid skills went virtually unnoticed.

The Policeman's Ball – 11 Beat

As Belle Vue Gardens made up a third of 11 Beat, it played a significant part in the policing of the area. In summertime, Blackpool was the playground of the north but, after the illuminations had been extinguished and the deckchairs stacked away, until late spring, it was the turn of Belle Vue, Manchester: zoological gardens, pleasure park, speedway, greyhound and stockcar racing, firework displays, championship boxing, international wrestling, orchestras and jazz bands, concerts and dancing.

To all this, add the two biggest social events of the year – the Railway Carnival and the Brass Band Championships and international stars of the calibre of Paul Robeson and Bob Hope and you have 11 Beat. How then does one set about describing it? Not just by portraying Belle Vue but, perhaps, by recounting events associated with it; a kaleidoscope of trivial happenings during my first two years of service, some of which I recall vividly, others less so.

At about one o'clock, one Friday morning, I had just stepped out of a darkened passageway, close to the Belle Vue Lake entrance. One didn't have to possess detective skills to realise that something was amiss, when a little boy looked over his shoulder and, on spotting you, hastily dashed into the ladies lavatories, as though it was a matter of considerable urgency. I allowed him a few moments, then went in after him. As would be expected at that time of night, all the cubicles were empty except one. I knocked on the bolted door.

"Come on, son, let's be having you."

He gave a few unconvincing grunts, rustled some paper about, flushed the toilet and came out with his excuses prepared.

"I'm sorry I had to use the Ladies, Sir, but I was taken short."

He was about nine or ten years old and his accent told me that he was a long way from home. Although he had a ready answer, there was something about him which was fundamentally honest and appealing.

"Where are you from, son?"

"Tooting, Sir."

"You're a long way from home."

"Yes, Sir. I've run away."

Close at hand was a small, green, painted cupboard.

"Empty your pockets and place the contents on top of that cupboard."

After inspecting his hands, I found them clean enough to eliminate him from suspicion of breaking offences. His possessions included some loose change and half a dozen speedway programmes.

"Follow the Aces (Belle Vue Speedway Aces) then?" I asked him, whilst examining one of the programmes.

"Yes, Sir. I've run away from home to see Jack Parker."

"Good rider, is he?" I asked, knowing the answer well enough.

"The bestest, Sir," he replied, before asking, "have you ever seen him?"

"Yes, many a time, son, but he doesn't ride at one o'clock in the morning. Well not round here he doesn't." I then became more serious. "Do your parents know where you are?"

"I don't know, Sir, they might."

"Haven't you told them?"

"No, Sir, but my brother knows where I am, he might have split."

There was nothing for it but to walk him to Gorton Section House.

"Present for you, Jim," I said to the Station Officer, "young Cockney lad, come to see the Aces."

"I've come to get Jack Parker's autograph," the kid corrected me.

In Hollywood they would have probably got Jack Parker out of bed to meet the youngster. He would have happily signed one of the lad's programmes, given him a ride on the back of his bike and then handed him a couple of complimentary tickets for the next meeting. Not us. We telephoned the police at Tooting and requested that his parents be sent to collect him. The youngster didn't seem too keen on the idea and made a point of letting me know. Cockney lads are more forward than their northern counterparts. Here, we would have called him a 'cheeky little sod' but in Tooting, he was probably thought of as being a bit chirpy. Or maybe he had seen the same Hollywood film and was disappointed when he came face to face with reality.

The men were in for their refreshments.

"When did you last eat, son?" I asked him.

"Dinnertime, Sir. I had a meat pie."

"Nothing since?"

He guessed what was coming his way.

"No, Sir," he rubbed his stomach as though it was hurting him, "I'm famished, Sir."

I brewed a jug of tea and handed him my sandwiches. He sat down at the table and opened them – boiled ham! Opposite him an old copper had just placed his supper down on the table – bacon, sausage, egg, tomato and fried bread. The youngster looked at his boiled ham sandwiches and then across at the cooked supper. I could read his mind, he was wanting to swap. I knew the old copper well. He wouldn't even have offered the kid a dipped buttie! I've seen many policemen give their sandwiches away in similar circumstances. Thirsty Fred, an Inspector with a drink problem, once gave his Christmas day lunch (turkey sandwiches, mince pies and Christmas cake) to a vagrant but, oddly enough, I have never seen a policeman give away a cooked meal.

"Get on with the butties," I advised him. "If you ask for a swap you could well end up on the losing side."

He bolted down the sandwiches and an hour later I heard from the police at Tooting that, although his father was none too pleased, his mother seemed relieved to know where he was and they would be there to collect him later on.

I was working from Gorton Section House with six months' service behind me and, although my numbers were not yet dry, at least my helmet was beginning to fit more comfortably. The Section Sergeant was quite a character, a rum and eccentric Yorkshireman named Arthur Palethorpe, who prided himself on being a bit of a card. It was a pleasure to work alongside him, for he refused to take life seriously and, when you are 20, and constantly dealing with other people's problems, it is nice to have a man like that around.

The first day that I met him, we were both sitting at the dining-room table having our refreshments. He screwed up one eye in a comical fashion and looked closely at my collar number.

"Ah, young Ninety-six. Smart boy, smart boy. Where are you from lad?"

"Stockport, Sarge, Cheshire."

He immediately forgave my parents for their lack of foresight.

"Nothing for you to be ashamed of, lad, you can't choose your place of birth. Yorkshire myself. The only county God can't improve on."

"Aye, good place to come from, Sarge, I'll give you that," I replied, "Bloody awful place to go to, though!"

He kept up the banter.

"Cheshire born and Cheshire bred, strong in th'arm and weak in th'ed."

I smiled. Indeed it was all I could do not to laugh at him. His eyes were twinkling merrily and I had not met a Sergeant like him before.

"Have you got the stale buns?" he asked next.

I looked at him inquisitively.

"The stale buns," he repeated, but I still looked nonplussed

"Stale buns, Sarge? I'm not with you."

He, in turn, pretended to look puzzled.

"You're the youngest man on the section aren't you?"

I nodded, still bemused as to what being young and inexperienced had to do with stale buns.

"Well, then, your Uncle Arthur's stale buns."

Uncle Arthur's stale buns meant as little to me as ordinary stale buns. "I'm still not with you, Sarge, you'll have to tell me more."

"Right, young man. When you've finished your breakfast, go to the cake shop. Tell them Sergeant Palethorpe's sent you and they'll give you a bag of stale buns."

I looked across at old Jim who was standing nearby and he confirmed the unusual instruction with a wink and a nod.

"When you've got them, you and your Uncle Arthur will go across to Belle Vue and feed the monkeys," Sergeant Palethorpe continued.

Anything is better than working a beat! No sooner had I finished my breakfast than I set off for the nearby cake shop where, it seemed, I was expected.

"Come for the Sergeant's buns have you?" asked the girl behind the counter with a pleasant smile. "They're all made up for you."

With that, she reached under the counter and extracted a large bag which she handed to me. I nodded and smiled.

"Is this a regular practice?"

The girl returned my smile.

"Never misses a day when he's working in this area. Come hail, rain or snow, Uncle Arthur always feeds the monkeys with the stale buns or stale bread." I thanked her and was leaving the shop when she called after me. "Sergeant Palethorpe is the nicest, kindest man I know, but doesn't he say some funny things?"

Later I accompanied the Sergeant to Belle Vue, his stick under his left arm and the buns in both hands. At ten o'clock in the morning, the place looked deserted.

"Now then, Sarge, got the buns hasta?" called an attendant, in his shirt sleeves, from a hut doorway some 50 yards away. "Come to see tha friends, hasta?" He came across to meet us and peeped into the large bag. "Bluddy 'ell," he spluttered, "curran' buns, scones and bluddy vanilla cuts. Tha's spoilin' buggars rotten, tha knows. Tha ought to give some a them to me, instead of to them little auld buggers."

Like Arthur, he was a Yorkshireman, but one more closely resembling his county's stereotype. Arthur immediately reverted to his native dialect and, to my ears, they may as well have been talking in tongues. After a couple of minutes they parted company and we continued past the elephant house, where two enormous African elephants stared at us and raised their trunks as we strolled by.

"Don't tha worry thaselves. I'll save thee both a vanilla cut," called out the Sergeant, "I'll be back in a few minutes."

Now he was mixing his Yorkshire accent with his adopted Manchester and was consequently a little easier to understand. They say that elephants never forget and these two certainly remembered their Uncle Arthur and knew what he had in the bag.

The monkey house was a large, caged dome, where the monkeys ran about freely and they must have heard the Sergeant when he was talking to the elephants, for they were all grouped together facing us, with their arms thrust through the bars. Arthur broke up the buns and pushed pieces into their open palms. The noise was terrific, pure bedlam.

180

After feeding them, we returned to the elephant house, where the two elephants were waiting, shifting their weight from one foot to the other, in their impatience to be fed. A deep, concrete trench separated us, so Arthur had to throw the vanilla cuts across to them.

Having exhausted our supply of stale buns, it was apparently time for important business and the Sergeant looked at me with a mock serious expression.

"Come on, young man, we can't stand here all day tha knows, there's work to be done."

As we left Belle Vue, I glanced at my watch. It had taken us just 20 minutes. Compared to some of the things which occurred later in my service, those 20 minutes could only be considered as trivial, and yet they provided a memory I will always cherish.

Before Dr Beeching's railway cuts, one of the two biggest social events on the Belle Vue calendar was The Railway Carnival, the other being the Brass Band Championship and each was held annually at the Gardens.

Although the band contest itself was held in the Kings Hall, for the first half of the day, much of the musical activity centred around the local pubs. Coaches carrying the bands would arrive in the area and then, by prior arrangement with the licensee, head for their chosen hostelry. Instruments would be unloaded and tuned, seating arrangements altered to suit the bandmaster and a temporary band practice room established. Once the whereabouts of the different bands became known, the surrounding district would be turned into a spontaneous music festival, as people flocked to listen to their favourite outfit, with some enthusiasts moving from pub to pub in order to assess each band's chances in the day's main event. In the midst of packed and appreciative audiences, the bandsmen would lubricate their throats and get in some last minute practice.

How astonishing it was to have all the country's top brass bands playing at the same time in one small area, admission free and ale at rock-bottom prices. The Black Dyke in The Plough, Fairey Aviation in the Gorton Brook, the CWS in the Midland and Brighouses nearly blowing the roof off at The Wagon and Horses. To me, being a keen brass band fan, I found it all enthralling.

Somewhere in the recesses of my mind, I have memories of a time when the carnival and the championship may have coincided. All day long, special trains pulled into both Belle Vue and Ashbury Stations, bringing railway employees from all parts of the country. Coaches unloaded at Belle Vue carpark, bringing the brass bands, their followers and endless crates of brown ale. This mix formed a good crowd and the day was one of great activity, much merriment and genuine musical ability and expertise.

The Railway Queen was elected and crowned, the brass band contest played and won and huge numbers of meat pies, sausage rolls and packets of crisps disappeared like snow in July, washed down by copious draughts of best ale. Children were lost, found and probably lost again, barrow boys were moved on, only to return, instrumentalists were running about carrying everything from a trumpet to a bass drum and girls wearing kiss-me-quick hats were trying their luck with the lads.

Looking after this lot was a police duty. I was on evening patrol, working from four until midnight and had joined in the carnival spirit quite early, controlling the traffic entering the coachpark at the back of the gardens, where the scene was chaotic. Realising it was impossible to work a traffic post with a lost child clutching my hand, bawling his head off, I left the motorists to their own devices and headed for the footpath. I was endeavouring to trace the child's parents, when I was approached by another lost soul; a middle-aged drunken Yorkshireman, with the most marvellous red face and blue-veined bulbous nose. Wearing a knotted white silk muffler, he was on the verge of losing his herringbone tweed cap, which hung perilously over one ear, like a burnt pancake. He wasn't just unsteady on his legs, he was almost out of his mind.

"Hasta seen Bingham's coach from Batley, lad?"

His breath almost rocked me back on my heels. But, worse, he had an unfortunate downward squint, which meant that whilst he was speaking to me, even though his face was pointing upwards, he ended up looking down at the child.

Surrounding us were hundreds of coaches, all packed within two feet of each other.

"Take your pick," I told him politely.

"Nay, tha'd know this one lad; it's a brown un with a yella stripe," whereupon he belched a cloud of beery fumes in my face.

I was saved from a further taste of the vapours, when a young woman rushed up to claim the child. She thanked me tearfully and was leading him away and scolding him, when she discovered that, not only had she found a son, but had also gained a friend. Clinging to the little boy's other hand, and walking along with them, was the lost Yorkshireman.

"Hasta seen Bingham's coach?" Receiving no reply, he continued more insistently, "Bingham's coach from Batley, brown un with a yella stripe. Hasta seen it, lass?"

The last thing I heard was her indignant reply.

"Er, not that I know of, Dad. I heard you the first time, but I thought you were talking to little Nigel."

It was an honest mistake if, perhaps, an unfortunate one and no doubt later she could have bitten her tongue off.

At 5.30 I was joined by a very fat elderly policeman, who waddled across the road from the coach park towards me. He was a C Division man, who must have been on the point of retirement, because I can't recall meeting him again and he wasn't a person you would forget in a hurry.

"Do you fancy a drink?" he asked, as if it was the sole purpose of his visit.

"I could murder a cup of tea," I replied.

Obviously this wasn't the answer he was expecting.

"Phew, I don't know if I can find you a cup of tea," he grunted, then quickly added in a kinder tone, "I'm very friendly with a party of people who have come by coach. They've left me a crate of beer on the back seat. You can have a bottle if you like."

I was so thirsty that I readily agreed and followed him as he waddled back across the road, into the crowded coach park. He led me through a maze of closely parked coaches and I saw that many of them had cases of bottled beer on the back seats. Suddenly, he disappeared into one declaring triumphantly, "This is it". Sure enough, on the back seat was a crate of brown ale. We sat, on either side of the coach, just in front of the back seats, where my colleague was able to swivel round and, with one hand, dexterously remove two bottles from the crate. Then, in true Baden Powell style, he reached into his breast pocket and produced his police whistle chain, attached to which, in lieu of the whistle, was an old-fashioned, cast-iron bottle opener. He effortlessly opened both bottles, handed one to me, drank the other, swivelled, produced two more and removed their caps. I had soon drunk two bottles but my friend had drunk five.

"Will you have another one?" he offered generously.

"No, thanks."

"Perhaps you're right, Ninety-six. Two's enough for anyone."

We left the coach and I made my way to the busiest area, feeling very uneasy about that old copper. Looking back, I could see him still waddling along between the rows of coaches.

After refreshments, the Inspector sent me to team up with Harry, of the knocker-up episode, to patrol inside Belle Vue Gardens, with instructions to keep a grip on things. There were two pairs of young policemen, all probationary constables, and we were kept extremely busy. If the duty roster was correct, then there should have been a few pairs of old coppers patrolling alongside us, but they had disappeared, as if off the face of the earth. No doubt they were comfortably ensconced somewhere, drinking and eating.

Just before ten o'clock, an attendant informed us that there was a, "right good fight going on outside the Kings Hall". Close to the rear of the hall, was a group of bandsmen who, from the appearance of their uniforms, all belonged to the same outfit. The two principal combatants were a trumpeter and a euphonium player. As we approached, the fight suddenly ended when the euphonium player's lips accidentally collided with his opponent's trumpet case. They started to swell immediately and it became clear, when they had reached the size of saucers, that their owner would neither be fighting, nor playing the euphonium for the next week or two.

I turned my attention to the trumpeter but need not have bothered. In the collision, the case had flown open and his trumpet flung to the ground. Unconcerned about his colleague's injuries, he had recovered his trumpet and was lovingly polishing it on his sleeve. I caught him by the arm, whilst the rest of the band gathered round.

"I'm going to put you out of Belle Vue," I warned him unceremoniously, "and if you dare to give me any trouble, I'll leave you to imagine what I'll do with that trumpet – blunt end first!" Not exactly the wording of a formal caution but he understood well enough, whilst the rest of the bandsmen found the words amusing.

As I led the trumpeter away to the nearest exit, the middle-aged bandmaster whispered to me over my shoulder.

"Are you locking him up, Officer?"

"No, I replied, "I'm just putting him out of the gardens."

"In that case, would you mind putting him out by the back gate? Only that's where our coach is parked and we've had enough for one day. We're ready for the off."

It is far easier to walk a man where he wants to go, so a quick change of direction saw us heading towards the coach park at the back. One or two of the bandsmen now entered into the spirit of the occasion because, as I marched their colleague out of the grounds, they followed behind playing Colonel Bogey.

As I ejected the trumpeter, the bandmaster approached me again. "Thanks a lot, Officer. I appreciate you could have locked him up, had you wanted to." Then he asked, "do you know what that bit of trouble was all about?"

"I would think the beer's had a bit to do with it," I suggested.

"Yes," he agreed, "we've all had a bit too much to drink but, in a way, it was the euphoniumist's fault. He's not practised as much as he should – he's been dodging the column. We were playing damn well in the championship until he hit a false note. It cost us a few points and that made the difference between winning and losing."

"Do you mean to say he collected that pair of lips for playing a wrong note?"

"Aye, daft isn't it?"

"Well, it's a good job your trumpet section has never heard me sing," I laughed, "I'd be terrified of the consequences."

The word, euphonium, stems from a Greek word meaning, 'sweet, soothing and kind'. Hearing the injured party cursing, moaning and threatening through his king-size lips, you wouldn't have thought so.

Just before midnight, approaching the end of a most unusual tour of duty, I was chatting to a diminutive bemedalled commissionaire who had fought in the First World War with the Manchester Bantams.

"It's been a busy day but most enjoyable," I told him.

"Aye, it has that, lad, but the carnivals are always good fun. The railway people are a nice crowd and the bobbies are a good bunch of lads too."

I was pleased with the last part of the observation but doubted its accuracy and conveyed my misgivings with as much humour as I could muster, recalling that most of the old coppers on duty had been conspicuous by their absence.

"Eeh lad, you should have seen it before t'war," he chuckled. "That's when the railway carnival really was the railway carnival."

I asked him whether it had been better than it was now.

"Eeh lad, much better, or worse, depends how you look at it, of course. There wasn't as much money flying about in those days and everyone seemed to be trying just that little bit harder. I remember the last one – last one before t'war that is. Now that was a real rum do, that was. I saw two of your lads going into the Tunnel of Love and I remember seeing one bobby take his helmet off and sit behind the motor-cyclist on the Wall of Death." Already having heard a little of what had gone on at Belle Vue in pre-war days, I told him that I wasn't too surprised. Not to be outdone, he added, "mind you, one or two of them went a bit too far."

At this, he stood back and waited to be prompted into more shocking revelations.

"Too far?" I obliged.

"Well, I'll tell you, lad," he confided in hushed tones. "There were two of 'em, they were in drink, mind you. You'll never guess, but they were feeding the elephants with teapot lids!"

Was it true, or had he been listening to one of Paddy's stories? Certainly I had heard Paddy tell of the heavy drinking, the Tunnel of Love, the Wall of Death and, yes, even of the teapot lids.

□ □ □ □

It was the big fight night at Belle Vue's Kings Hall. Top of the bill may have been either former world light heavyweight champion, Freddie Mills, or future world middleweight champion, Randolf Turpin. I was with a Sergeant helping to control the thousands of boxing fans flocking towards the main entrance to the gardens. It was a warm night and the fans were coming from all directions, converging on the narrow turnstiles with that characteristic look of excitement and expectancy, which is peculiar to those who follow boxing and other forms of blood sport.

As always, on such big occasions, the atmosphere seemed charged with electricity, as if there was a summer storm brewing. Taxis drew up and cigar-smoking dandies assisted fur-coated women to alight and even they had that lustful look on their rouged faces.

Hurrying towards us, the fans paused to surround the white-coated attendants, clamouring for programmes, whilst glancing first at their watches and then at their friends, impatiently waiting nearby. Watching all of this you would have thought that they only had seconds to spare, instead of the 60 minutes before the first bout. Men with bent noses and cauliflower ears, gossiped close to the entrances, hoping to be recognised by the bookies pushing their way through and preparing to treat them like royalty, should they be lucky enough to receive a five shilling tip.

Suddenly, as if some hidden power was drawing him towards the arena, bobbing and weaving his way through the crowd, emerged a small, solitary figure. He paused in his slow jogging, his head swaying from side to side like a striking cobra, whilst he shadow-boxed with an imaginary opponent. He ignored the people who called out to him, concentrating on his own actions.

First he jabbed with a clenched left fist, swayed his body, hooked viciously with his left, then crossed with a fast right to a fancied head. Still ignoring those gathered around, he danced back and circled his invisible adversary, jabbing out a whole series of straight lefts, before once again starting to jog towards us. He stopped a few yards away and commenced skipping at an incredible speed then, seeing us, he still kept his guard up, whilst he shuffled in.

He stopped in front of me, bobbing and feinting, shoulders constantly moving and then he threw a flurry of punches to my body, pulling each one so that it wouldn't land. I smiled at him, but he looked back at me without expression, continuing to throw punches, whilst staring at me through dull, slightly glazed eyes. He was poetry in motion, a mixture of speed, style, grace and whipcord strength.

"OK, Jackie," said the Sergeant.

The little man paused, looked at the Sergeant, gave a shake of his head and then, retracing his steps, started jogging and shadow-boxing until he was lost from view in the milling crowd.

"Do you know who that was?" asked the Sergeant.

I nodded sadly. It was Jackie Brown, former flyweight champion of the world. He was about 38 years of age.

Soon both Freddie Mills and Randolf Turpin, both lion-hearted men, were to commit suicide. These facts speak for themselves and do not commend boxing as a sport.

One can hardly classify all-in-wrestling as a blood sport. If blood does flow, it is usually the result of two heads accidentally colliding, or when one of the wrestlers puts his nose in the wrong place, at the wrong time. Wrestling is a gymnastic performance which, when seen from a distance and executed by two accomplished athletes, can look very convincing, particularly if they are vociferous in their appeals for mercy or submission, or have elastic faces, which can register the effects of pain and anguish. Unfortunately, the telescopic use of television cameras has revealed much of its duplicity but, in those days, even if they couldn't fool all of the people, all of the time, they at least fooled some of the people, some of the time. That is, all the people who went along to watch the performance.

It was the main bout of the evening. The referee was Dick the Dormouse, the goodie was Karel Istav, a handsome blonde giant with a marvellous body and the features of Kirk Douglas; he was the envy of every man present and the darling of every woman from 16 to 60. The baddie was the mysterious Baron Brutelli, a masked villain from some far distant land; an evil colossus who would only take off his mask and reveal his face when beaten in combat.

As far as the pretend villainy was concerned, Baron Brutelli had fully lived up to his reputation and had given Istav a real working over. Mumbling and cursing in a foreign tongue, he had continuously fouled Karel, punching and kicking him where it hurt most and elbowing him in the face whenever possible. Now, having received his third and final warning, he had delighted the male spectators but incensed every woman in the hall, by punching Karel with a closed fist, making his nose bleed.

At two minutes to nine, the time when, each week, the programme ended, Dick the Dormouse disqualified the Baron, amidst a terrible uproar. I was standing in the central aisle, leading to the dressing room, when the Baron strode majestically away from the ring. All around me the women were going wild, some almost berserk, as Karel ducked out of the ring, his head swathed in a blood-stained towel.

"You dirty swine, Baron. Fight like an Englishman, you bugger."

"Get your flaming mask off, you rotten foreigner."

"He'd beat you every time if you fought fair."

"You Bulgarian bastard."

As the Baron retreated to the dressing room, amidst this shower of abuse, a woman rushed at him, aiming blows with her umbrella. The Baron snatched it from her, handed it back and, from behind the mask, called out in perfect English, with a northern accent:

"Now piss off with thee, missis, or I'll tan thee arse for thee."

□ □ □ □

When controlling traffic, there is nothing a policeman finds more annoying than an impatient driver sounding his horn behind his back. It is usually some self-opinionated twit, who thinks he is a cut above the rest; a man not used to being kept waiting with the common herd. You could either ignore him, or you could walk across to him, point out that it is an offence to sound a car horn when stationary and then book him. Being stubborn, I always chose to ignore such people and it was amazing how long I could manage to keep them waiting.

There had been a large political rally at the Kings Hall. The guest speaker was Sir Anthony Eden, destined to become a Tory Prime Minister. It was understood that, after the rally, Sir Anthony would leave by the rear exit, with a police escort. The rally was over and I had been relegated to controlling the traffic outside Belle Vue's main entrance, a much busier post, but well out of the official limelight. I had allowed a long stream of cars to leave the gardens and then, halting their flow, turned to regulate the movement of traffic along the main Hyde Road, where two long double lines of stationary vehicles had built up.

No sooner had I turned my back on the cars still waiting to come out of Belle Vue Gardens, than someone behind me sounded his horn. I felt my back stiffen. Here we go again! Even though I was young and inexperienced, I knew full well that far more self-opinionated car owners were likely to attend the Conservative rallies than those of the Socialists or Liberals.

"Peep, peep."

I just ignored it.

"Peep, peep."

"Again I kept my back turned.

"Peep, peep."

"You can keep that up all day," I thought.

It's amazing, if counting, how many peeps can be sounded in five minutes – perhaps as many as 50, or even 60, if trying hard enough. I finally relented and, keeping a straight face, as though unaware of the pandemonium behind me, I turned to face the nuisance, which turned out to be a chauffeur-driven limousine. Under his peaked cap, the chauffeur's face was almost purple. In the back of the car was Sir Anthony Eden. I saluted him smartly but he didn't acknowledge the salute, or even my presence, but looked straight through me. His face looked ashen, as though he was very tired and not a little put out.

□ □ □ □

The C Division's main social event was the annual dance which, in county or borough circles, would have been referred to by its more dignified title of the Police Ball. But, as Shakespeare himself wrote, "What's in a name? That which we call a rose, by any other name would smell as sweet". And, indeed, if one compared our 'do' with many a shire county police ball, it would come out the clear winner.

At Belle Vue we had one of the country's top ballrooms. The orchestra was always one of the best and not of the, 'Billy Buttercup and his Five Swinging Petals' variety. The Superintendent was personally responsible for the arrangements and he was a belt and braces man, who left nothing to chance.

Everyone was immaculately turned out, with a fair sprinkling of evening suits in evidence. From the married policeman's point of view, it was an event he could easily afford, admission being two shillings (ten pence), including refreshments and free beer. It gave his wife the opportunity to dress up and meet a few friends. For the young, unattached policeman, it was an evening not to be missed. The Administration Department sent a few tickets to Ancoats Hospital and a group of young nurses would arrive at about 8.30 and laugh amongst themselves at the latest warning issued by the Matron. Together, the young ones never failed to make it a rumbustious affair, with the evening in full swing from about 9pm, until the 'carriages arrived' at one o'clock in the morning. By comparison, the typical shire county police ball, and certainly the one I went to, was more like a political meeting, set to music.

From the Superintendent's standpoint, and this is important, for it was he who worked harder than anyone to make it a success, it was a chance to show off his men under what he hoped would be the most favourable conditions, under the strict control of their wives or sweethearts, for he was inclined to worry in case things went wrong. To allay some of these worries, he took an immense interest in the careful preparations, ensuring that there were enough canteen profits to pay for the refreshments and the beer, seeing to it that there was good liaison with the Belle Vue staff and that the orchestra was booked well in advance.

Then there had to be the utmost discretion as to which guests were invited. "I don't want any bloody paymasters coming along," he would say over and over again; and he was not referring to army paymasters. Which now left him with only the young ones to worry about and, somehow, he always found himself at cross purposes with them. He wanted the dance to be the social success of the year, whilst they were determined to enjoy themselves, no matter what. Having been born in the reign of Queen Victoria, he believed in regimentation, was not considered to be enlightened and, like Victor Sylvester, was a strict tempo man, not only in his choice of music, but in all things he considered proper.

For him, the best part of the evening was undoubtedly when, by tradition, he and his wife would be invited to start the proceedings with the first waltz. With old-world courtesy, he would escort her onto the dance floor, bow, then gracefully lead her for a full circuit of the ballroom, before other dancers gradually joined them. Afterwards, he would be on pins for, based on his experience from other years, he expected something to go wrong.

Even though there were three licensed bars and a room where free ale was allocated, he knew that some of the young ones would have met as early as 5.30 in the evening at the Three Arrows and that a few of them would already have had more than enough by the time they arrived to sample the free beer.

The nurses had been invited, he'd seen to that, but would Staff Nurse Phoebe, the benevolent girl they called Freebie, arrive? She was a star turn and dispensed her favours faster than she did the bloody medicine. And would that policewoman from headquarters put in an appearance with her special friend? He could well do without the two of them prancing around the dance floor in their ballgowns, having the time of their life, at his expense.

Phoebe would be the first nurse to both receive and accept an invitation – he could live with that and besides there was nothing he could do about it. But there would be trouble if any of the lads started buggering about with the animals, like they did last year. Three hours he'd spent answering complaints about those bloody screeching monkeys and no wonder. Would Dovey, his man of many parts and now the barman, dish out too much free beer? Would any of the silly probationers disgrace themselves and fall over or, even worse, be sick?

After his mind had run riot on all the foreseeable difficulties, he would try to deal with the problems before they even arose and soon became so agitated that he would jump to his feet:

"Excuse me, my dear," he would whisper to his wife, "I must have a quick word with Mr Dovey in the back room."

He had a heart of gold and it was a pity that by worrying unduly, he tended to spoil his own evening. We young ones couldn't see why it mattered if Phoebe was round the back with one of our mates? Good for Phoebe – and it was said she danced all the better afterwards! If half a dozen of the lads had got tanked up and were rowing a group of young nurses round the boating lake – so what? No one needed to let their hair down more than the nurses from Ancoats Hospital. Besides, the lake wasn't deep enough for anyone to drown in, even if one of the boats did capsize. If Joe's jokes were getting a bit too near the knuckle – so what? His wife would sort him out when she got him home. No one was going to upset the monkey house this year; last year had been a one off. Surely he had over-reacted when he threatened to issue passouts. Christ! He'll be wanting to stamp our wrists with indelible ink next. Sure, there will be a few who will get well and truly plastered and the odd one or two will be unsteady on their feet. Someone is bound to be ill after all that rich food, but no one would get nasty, they never did. All these things added spice to the evening for us.

This year, for me, the dance was going to be different. I had taken a lovely girl along with me, a girl who, although I didn't know it then, was a friend of my future wife. I intended to be on my best behaviour, to remain relatively sober and, in order to achieve this, I had promised to stay in the company of Harry and his young wife and not to make so many trips to the bar.

When, at 10pm, the young bloods rolled in from the Three Arrows, conspicuous in their company, was the joyous Phoebe, leading Ben Nevis, a towering and craggy young Scot, into the ballroom. Ben had recently been recruited from the Outer Hebrides, where his head must have been permanently shrouded in mist. As yet, he had no conception of the term social drinking and had been consuming whisky at the same rate as the others had been drinking beer!

Having decided to remain relatively sober, I was determined to give them a wide berth but, because I had friends in the group, it was difficult, especially as my partner was rather attractive and a succession of drunken friends all wanted to be introduced. Even so, I handled it pretty well.

Then came the last waltz. At the first sound of the music I led my partner onto the dance floor, as sober as a High Court Judge. In one corner, Phoebe was still claiming Ben Nevis as her own. Although it was the last waltz, Ben was doing a variation of a long-forgotten Gaelic reel, which required acres upon acres of space, whilst Phoebe, as game as ever, was facing him and dancing what appeared to be a very slow jitterbug. Clustered behind them, clapping in time to the music and egging them on, was the rest of the group. Every few seconds the Gaelic reel cum Jitterbug called for Ben to catch hold of his partner, twirl her round and then throw her out with skirts flying, whilst still holding onto her with one hand. Ben had obviously discovered that there were worse experiences than grabbing hold of Phoebe who, in turn, wasn't raising any serious objection when his hand occasionally missed her waist by a few inches and landed where it shouldn't.

I waltzed my partner sedately round the edge of the floor until I arrived at Ben's corner. With room to spare, I went into what should have been an elegant spin turn, if it hadn't coincided with one of Ben's more enthusiastic twirls and throwouts, in which he spun the voluptuous Phoebe towards us, completely out of control. In taking evasive action, I pulled away too sharply, overbalanced and fell to the floor, pulling my partner down on top of me. Three of the group almost fell over themselves as they raced to remove her from my arms. Phoebe bent to my assistance, leaving Ben Nevis jigging about like a loose telegraph pole, left arm fully outstretched and gawping about him with his mouth wide open, as he sought to locate his partner. Phoebe laughed out loud and was hauling me to my feet when the Superintendent came waltzing regally by in time to the music of the Whiffenpoof Song. Still on the alert for anything that might ruin his night, he glared over his wife's shoulder and adding two and two together to make five, barked out:

"Ninety-six – my office – nine o'clock tomorrow morning!"

Those laying claim to my partner found this hilarious, particularly when they tried to explain my predicament. I stood, with Phoebe still clutching my hand, aware that behind me Ben had lost his concentration and, with feet glued to the spot, was wobbling precariously, ready to topple at any moment. In front of me, a sea of smiling faces floated past, whilst in the background the band played soft and low. On the stage, the crooner stepped forward to lean into the mike and with a sad expression spreading over his face, took up the lyrics in a melancholy voice.

"Poor little lambs who have lost their way, ba-ba-ba,

Little black sheep who have gone astray, ba-ba-ba."

He had summed up my probationary period on the 'C' more appropriately than I ever could.